SNOOKER
PLAYER BY PLAYER

SNOOKER
PLAYER BY PLAYER

First published in the UK in 2013

www.demand-media.co.uk

Printed and bound in China

ISBN 978-1-909217-45-4

CONTENTS

Introduction

Right: *An illustration of students playing three-ball pocket billiards in Tübingen, Germany, in the early 19th century*

It is widely held that an early version of snooker was played in the latter part of the 19th century by British army officers in India, but the game can race its roots back to the Middle Ages. Cue sports like billiards had been evolving from the mid-14th century when an outdoor game similar to croquet morphed into an indoor table game played by, amongst others, King Louis XI of France.

The outdoor variant then evolved separately into modern croquet, golf, cricket and various bowling games, while the indoor version grew so popular that by the mid-18th century it was being played in almost every café in Paris. The rather wieldy mace that had been used to strike the ball was refined into a delicate cue by 1800, and stuffed cushions were then added to stop the wooden balls falling off the table. Little scoring arches like croquet hoops were then swapped for pockets, the balls were upgraded to ivory and the game of billiards as we know it today was established.

In around 1874 coloured balls were added to the reds and black during a game of billiards at the officers' mess in Jabalpur. Ten years later, Sir Neville Chamberlain of the Devonshire Regiment (not the 20th-century prime minister) was playing an inexperienced opponent who failed to pot a ball after a shot. Chamberlain, probably because the word 'snooker' was slang for a new recruit, labelled him thus, and novice billiard players from then on were known as snookers.

Chamberlain drew up a set of rules that differentiated between billiards and the new game with its various coloured balls, and its popularity spread back to the UK and throughout the Commonwealth. In the early part of the 20th century it was still a game for the privileged few who could afford a table, however, but it gradually

filtered down to the working men's clubs.

By 1927 the game had become so popular that professional English billiards champion Joe Davis helped found the World Championship. He dominated the event for the next two decades and was unbeaten until his retirement in 1946. The game declined in the 1950s and early 1960s and it wasn't until David Attenborough, then working as the controller of BBC2, commissioned a series called Pot Black (to promote colour television) that the sport was brought to a wider audience.

The experiment was a huge success and a new World Championship was introduced. By 1977 the sport had moved to its spiritual home, the Crucible Theatre in Sheffield, and the following year the event was televised in its entirety. Snooker's popularity increased rapidly and colourful characters like Alex Higgins, Jimmy White, Bill Werbeniuk, Dennis Taylor, John Virgo and Steve Davis helped reel in up to 18 million TV viewers for epic matches like the 1985 world final.

Steve Davis dominated the decade but the 1990s would belong to a prodigiously talented Scotsman, Stephen Hendry. More recently, Ronnie O'Sullivan, John Higgins, Neil Robertson, Mark Selby, Judd Trump and Mark Williams have all battled it out for the coveted world number one spot. The game has also become hugely popular in the Far East, with the Chinese in particular threatening to dominate the sport for the next generation.

Above: *Billiards in the early 18th century bears little resemblance to the game of today*

Advani

Below: *Pankaj Advani at the 2012 Paul Hunter Classic*

Pankaj Advani was coached from a young age by former national champion Arvind Savur. He won his first title at the age of 12 and was prolific at both snooker and billiards – he was Indian Junior Billiards Champion in 2000 and 2001, and champion of both cue sports in 2003. In 2005 he achieved the Grand Double of the 'time' and 'points' formats at the World Billiards Championship, and he is the only person to win all five major billiards events in one season. He then won the World Professional Billiards Title by demolishing nine-time champion Mike Russell.

Having been offered a wildcard spot on the main snooker tour, he promptly dispatched Craig Steadman, Steve Davis, Alan McManus and Michael Holt during qualifying for the International Championship, but he then withdrew from the event to defend his billiards world crown (successfully). He then beat John Higgins 4-1 on the PTC tour and reached the quarter-final of the 2013 Welsh Open with a win over Graeme Dott, although he eventually lost to Judd Trump. If he can bring his exceptional billiard skills to the snooker table, there's no reason why he can't challenge for ranking titles in the near future.

Name: Pankaj Advani
Born: July 24th 1985, Maharashtra
Nationality: Indian
Turned Pro: 2003
Century Breaks: 10
Highest Break: 143
Ranking Titles: 0
World Titles: 0

Allen

Mark Allen benefited from Lottery funding, which helped him win the Northern Ireland Championships at Under-14, 16 and 19 levels. He then entered an invitational event in his home country and beat Steve Davis and John Higgins before eventually losing to Stephen Hendry in the quarter-final.

In his third professional season he reached the last 32 of the UK Championships, and he also made an impact at the 2006 Welsh Open. He threw away a lead over Shaun Murphy, however, and he then surrendered another winning position to Andy Hicks at the qualifying tournament for that year's World Championships.

His fortunes were about to change, however. In 2007 he qualified for his first World Championships, and he discarded his choker's tag by beating former champion Ken Doherty in the first round. He eventually lost to an inspired Matthew Stevens but by then he was already ranked in the top 32.

Doherty branded him a disgrace at the 2007 Grand Prix when he twice struck the cushion with his fist, but Allen survived the repercussions and gradually clawed his way into the top 16 with wins over Graeme Dott and Ryan Day. In 2009 he defeated defending champion Ronnie O'Sullivan at the World Championships but he eventually lost 13-17 to John Higgins in the semi-final. He won his first tournament – the Jiangsu Classic – later that year, demolishing home favourite Ding Junhui 6-0 in the final.

At the 2010 World Championships he was on course for a maximum break when he came unstuck on the green. He later recorded the tournament's first 146 break when he beat Mark Davis in the second round. He made it to his first ranking event final at the 2011 UK Championships (after five previous attempts) but, despite a determined fight-back from a desperate position, Judd Trump held on to win 10-8.

He finally won his first ranking tournament at the World Open in China by beating Jimmy Robertson, Judd Trump, Mark King, Mark Selby and Steven Lee, but the season ended in disappointment

Above: *Mark Allen pots the black at the 2012 Paul Hunter Classic*

after first-round losses at the China Open and 2012 World Championships.

Allen seems to court controversy with the snooker establishment. He has long-running and bitter feuds with Stuart Bingham and Ken Doherty, and he also called for the chairman of the World Professional Billiards & Snooker Association, Barry Hearn, to resign after he changed the format of some tournaments and encouraged the crowds to be more vocal. He also criticised the conditions in China for the World Open and was promptly fined. He then accused several of the Chinese players of not owning up to fouls, for which he was again fined by the WPBSA.

Allen lost in the first round of the 2013 World Championship to Mark King.

Name: Mark Allen
Born: February 22nd 1986, Antrim
Nationality: Northern Irish
Turned Pro: 2003
Century Breaks: 176
Highest Break: 146
Ranking Titles: 2
World Titles: 0

Bingham

Stuart Bingham had a reputation as a journeyman who never quite reached his potential, but an upsurge in his recent fortunes has seen him enter the top 16. In 1996 he won the English and World Amateur titles but he didn't make an impact in a professional tournament until the 1999 Welsh Open, where he beat John Higgins on the way to the quarter-final. The following season he caused a major upset when he defeated Stephen Hendry in the first round of the World Championships while he was only just ranked in the world's top 100.

In 2002 he enjoyed more success at the game's blue riband event when he almost made a maximum break (he came unstuck on the final pink). Having missed out on £147,000 he then lost a match he should have won (8-10) to Ken Doherty. From 2004 until 2006 Bingham was solid if not spectacular. He reached the quarter-final of the Grand Prix by beating then world champion Shaun Murphy and made the same stage at the UK Championship. He then made a 147 in the qualifying tournament for the Masters and beat Steve Davis in the event itself.

Above: *Stuart Bingham uses the rest at the 2011 Shanghai Masters*

Bingham remains on the fringes of the world's elite and occasionally causes a shock, such as when he defeated Ronnie O'Sullivan 9-6 at the 2010 UK Championship. He finally won his first ranking event in 2011 when he came from 8-5 down to beat Mark Williams in the Australian Goldfields Open, but he then performed poorly for the remainder of the season.

He made a great start to the 2012/13 season, however, winning his first two tournaments and then making the final of the Wuxi Classic ranking event. In the final itself he made his third competitive 147 but he couldn't stop Ricky Walden ending his 16-match unbeaten streak and taking the title. He also performed well at the 2013 World Championships, reaching the quarter-final before being beaten by eventual winner Ronnie O'Sullivan.

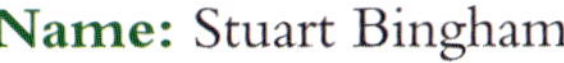

Name: Stuart Bingham
Born: May 21st 1976, Basildon
Nationality: English
Turned Pro: 1995
Century Breaks: 158
Highest Break: 147
Ranking Titles: 1
World Titles: 0

Bond

Right: *Nigel Bond*

Nigel Bond enjoyed a sterling amateur career before he turned professional in 1989. He reached a ranking semi-final in his first pro season and then made the final of the 1990 Grand Prix. This was the Hendry era, however, and Bond was soundly beaten 10-5 by the Scotsman.

The pair met again in the final of the 1995 World Championship but Hendry was again too strong and he ran out a comfortable 18-9 winner. The year before Bond had pulled off one of the tournament's greatest comebacks when he rallied from 9-2 down to beat Cliff Thorburn 10-9 in the Canadian's last Crucible appearance. Now ranked in the world's top five, he won his only ranking title to date, the 1996 British Open, by beating John Higgins after he needed a snooker in the final frame.

Between 1993 and 1996 Hendry proved to be his nemesis at every World Championship, but Bond eventually scored a victory over the master in their Crucible quarter-final in 2006. Bond led comfortably but was then pegged back to 7-7. He eventually managed to pot a re-spotted black (the first to decide the final frame of a World Championship match) to record his first win at the event in seven years.

In 2011, Bond won a one-frame shootout tournament for the world's top 64 players, but he has since slipped down the rankings and is now outside the top 32.

Name: Nigel Bond
Born: November 15th 1965, Darley Dale
Nationality: English
Turned Pro: 1989
Century Breaks: 99
Highest Break: 140
Ranking Titles: 1
World Titles: 0

Brecel

Luca Brecel is surely one of snooker's future stars. In 2009, aged only 14, he became the youngest European Under-19 Champion. He then beat Jimmy White and Ken Doherty in the World Series of Snooker before narrowly losing to Graeme Dott in the quarter-final. He also beat Joe Perry in the Paul Hunter Classic and Stephen Hendry in an exhibition in Bruges.

In 2010 he became Belgian Champion and he eventually turned professional after being offered a wildcard on the main tour the following year. By the end of the season he was ranked 65 in the world and he made his first 147 at an amateur event. In 2012 he broke another record when he beat Ian McCulloch, Barry Pinches, Michael Holt and Mark King to become the youngest person to qualify for the World Championship. Despite knocking in a century, he was defeated in the first round by Stephen Maguire.

He found the rest of the season tough but he then won four qualifying matches to reach the main draw for the 2012 UK Championship. He continued his good form by seeing off Ricky Walden (6-5) and Mark King (6-4) to become the first Belgian to reach the quarter-final of a ranking event. He had two chances to beat Shaun Murphy in his next match but couldn't pot a relatively easy pink and lost 6-5.

Given time to mature and learn how to grind out results when things aren't going his way, Brecel will surely be a force in the game for the next two decades.

Left: *Luca Brecel could dominate snooker for a generation*

Name: Luca Brecel
Born: March 8th 1995, Dilsen-Stokkem
Nationality: Belgian
Turned Pro: 2011
Century Breaks: 22
Highest Break: 136
Ranking Titles: 0
World Titles: 0

Burnett

Right: *Jamie Burnett attempts a tricky long pot with the rest*

It took Jamie Burnett four years to make an impact on the professional tour when he reached his first World Championships. Despite leading Terry Griffiths 5-0 in the opening round he capitulated and lost 10-9. He then reached the quarter-finals of the 1997 German Open and the 1998 Grand Prix. The following season he beat world number one Stephen Hendry twice and also recorded victories over Stephen Lee and Mark Williams.

During qualifying for the 2004 UK Championship, opponent Leo Fernandez fouled and the referee awarded Burnett a free ball. He potted the brown as an extra red and then cleared the table with a break of 148, the first time anyone had exceeded the 'maximum' in a professional tournament.

He was embroiled in a betting controversy when huge amounts of money were placed on him losing 3-9 to Stephen Maguire at the 2008 UK Championships but, although he was questioned by police, they found no evidence of wrongdoing by either player. He qualified for the 2009 World Championship after a record absence of 13 years, and then reached his first ranking final in Shanghai after impressive wins over Andrew Higginson, Mark Davis and Jamie Cope, although Ali Carter beat him in the final itself, 10-7.

He failed to qualify for any ranking event in 2011/12 but began 2012/13 strongly and almost won his first title at the minor-ranking Gdynia Open. Neil Robertson held on to win a tense final 4-3, however. He then failed to win a match from December onwards and missed out on qualifying for the 2013 World Championship.

Name: Jamie Burnett
Born: September 16th 1975, Glasgow
Nationality: Scottish
Turned Pro: 1992
Century Breaks: 109
Highest Break: 148
Ranking Titles: 0
World Titles: 0

Campbell

Above: *Marcus Campbell eyes a long pot at the Paul Hunter Classic*

Marcus Campbell made little impact on the world of snooker until an extraordinary match at the 1998 UK Championship. Stephen Hendry was the game's dominant force and he was expected to trounce Campbell, but the underdog recorded one of the most surprising results not just in snooker but in any sport when he thrashed Hendry 9-0. He proved the result was no fluke by beating Quinten Hann 9-6 in the next round.

Campbell couldn't reach the same heights until he beat Graeme Dott and Anthony Hamilton at the 2007/08 Grand Prix, although he eventually lost to Joe Swail. He also showed strongly at the Welsh Open with wins over Lee Spick, Ricky Walden and Gerard Greene, before he lost to Ding Junhui. He qualified as a wildcard for the 2008 Bahrain Championship with a 147 but was beaten in the tournament by eventual champion Neil Robertson. He then qualified for the 2010 World Championship but couldn't get past Mark Williams.

Campbell won the Euro Players Tour Championship, a minor-ranking tournament, in 2010 in a season that saw him enter the world's top 32. In 2011/12 he entered six of the eight ranking tournaments but lost at the last 16 stage and only finished the season 30th in the order of merit. In 2012/13 Campbell qualified for the Wuxi Classic and reached the semi-final at a ranking tournament for the first time in his career by beating Stephen Lee, Fergal O'Brien and Mark Williams. He eventually succumbed to nerves and lost 1-6 to Ricky Walden, although a ranking win is probably within his grasp.

He lost to an inspired Ronnie O'Sullivan in the first round of the 2013 World Championship.

Name: Marcus Campbell
Born: September 22nd 1972, Dumbarton
Nationality: Scottish
Turned Pro: 1991
Century Breaks: 55
Highest Break: 147
Ranking Titles: 0
World Titles: 0

Carter

Below: *Ali Carter is a picture of concentration*

Far Right: *Bob Chaperon (right) with Cliff Thorburn*

Ali Carter turned professional in 1996 but it was three years before he made his mark on the game when he won the Benson & Hedges Championship and was voted the year's best young player. He then reached the semi-final of the 1999 Grand Prix but his early promise soon tapered off and he didn't make another semi until the 2007 Malta Cup. He also couldn't break into the elite top 16 until 2006, but he backed up solid performances with a good run at the 2007 World Championship, where he beat Andy Hicks and Stephen Hendry.

He enjoyed another strong showing at the 2008 event and beat Barry Hawkins (in a final frame decider), world number one Shaun Murphy, 2002 champion Peter Ebdon, and then Joe Perry in the semi-final. He also made his first maximum break. Having booked his place against Ronnie O'Sullivan, Carter couldn't stop the rocket from claiming the title with a convincing 18-8 win.

He finally won his first ranking event, the 2009 Welsh Open, after victories over Jimmy White, Graeme Dott, Shaun Murphy, Anthony Hamilton and Joe Swail. Strong showings at the back end of 2009/10 saw him move up to fourth in the world rankings, and he then won the Shanghai Masters. His next season was poor by comparison and he even contemplated retirement after dropping out of the world's top 16.

Having adjusted his diet to try combating Crohn's disease, Carter returned to the World Championship and demolished Mark Davis 10-2. He then masterminded an incredible comeback against Judd Trump to win 13-12, before beating debutant Jamie Jones and then Stephen Maguire. He saw off the Scotsman 17-12 to book his second world final appearance against Ronnie O'Sullivan, but he couldn't stop O'Sullivan taking the match 18-11.

In 2013 Carter won his third ranking event, the German Masters, and with nearly a million pounds earned during his career he is now back in the world's top 16. He also ran into Ronnie O'Sullivan at the 2013 World Championship and was beaten 8-13 in the second round.

Name: Ali Carter
Born: July 25th 1979, Colchester
Nationality: English
Turned Pro: 1996
Century Breaks: 143
Highest Break: 147
Ranking Titles: 3
World Titles: 0

Chaperon

Bob Chaperon will forever be remembered as the outsider who beat Alex Higgins 10-8 in the final of the 1990 British Open. He was one of several top Canadian players alongside Cliff Thorburn, Alain Robidoux, Kirk Stevens and Bill Werbeniuk, and was part of the team that won the World Cup for his country in 1990. He was national champion in 1981 and 2000 but the 1990s saw him slip down the world rankings and he retired in 2001. In 2010, however, he took the Alain Robidoux Invitational event after a two-year lay-off. He still plays on the North American circuit in pro/am charity tournaments.

Name: Bob Chaperon
Born: May 18th 1958
Nationality: Canadian
Turned Pro: 1984 – 2001
Century Breaks: 10
Highest Break: 132
Ranking Titles: 1
World Titles: 0

Charlton

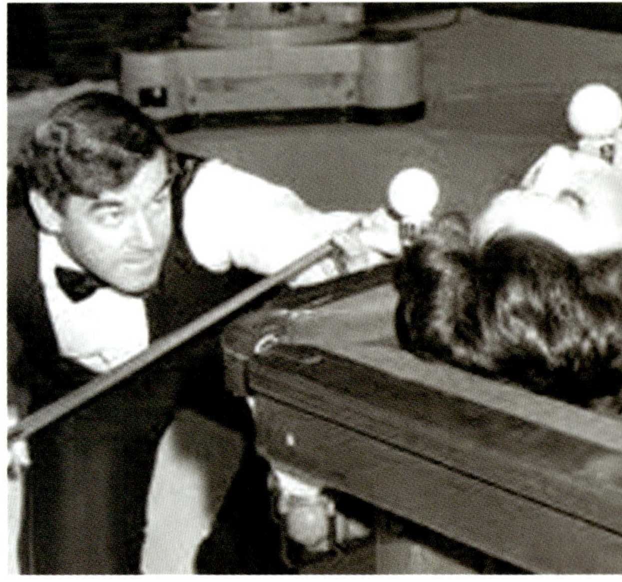

Right: *Eddie Charlton lines up a trick shot*

Eddie Charlton came from a sporting family that included brother Jim, who was also a snooker player, although he never turned professional. Charlton could have made it as a footballer, surfer, cricketer or boxer but he chose snooker and billiards instead (he carried the Olympic torch before the 1956 Melbourne Games).

He won his first billiard title, the Australian Professional Championship, a year after turning pro, and with only one exception he would win it every year for the next two decades. In 1974 and 1976 he finished runner up to Rex Williams, and fell agonisingly short in his third world billiards final in 1984. Four years later he made the final for the last time, but Norman Dagley took the title.

His snooker career was equally impressive: he was ranked in the top three for five years from 1976, and reached the world final on three occasions, in 1968, 1973 and 1975, although he lost each time. In 1972, 1973 and 1980 he won BBC television's Pot Black tournament, and he also took the 1976 World Matchplay title.

Charlton played with a straight and simple action and was the most successful Australian player until Neil Robertson. He made his last Crucible appearance in 1992 (in a 10-0 defeat by defending champion John Parrott), retired in 1995 and died in 2004 in Palmerston North following an operation.

Name: Eddie Charlton
Born: October 21st 1929, New South Wales
Died: November 7th 2004, New Zealand
Nationality: Australian
Turned Pro: 1963 - 1995
Highest Break: 124
Ranking Titles: 0
World Titles: 0

Cope

Above: *Jamie Cope*

Jamie Cope showed promise as a junior but after two poor years he almost vanished. In the 2004/05 season, however, he made a comeback on the Challenge Tour for emerging players and won two tournaments. Back on the main tour he reached the last 16 of the Grand Prix, the Welsh Open and the China Open, and he also registered wins over Joe Perry, Steve Davis and John Parrott.

In 2005 he became the first player in history to achieve a verified 155 break (after a foul by an opponent, a colour can be used as a free ball, which counts as an extra red), although it was only during a practice frame and not in a tournament proper. The following year he made a 147 at the Grand Prix, but he lost in the final (5-9) to Neil Robertson.

A couple of mediocre seasons followed and he didn't make it to the World Championships until 2008. He lost to Peter Ebdon in the first round but recovered from the setback to record a second maximum at the Shanghai Masters against Mark Williams. He surrendered a two-frame lead to John Higgins at the 2009 World Championship and was left outside the top 16, but he finally joined the elite players in 2010/11 by reaching the semi-final at the Masters.

He dropped back down the rankings after a poor start to the next season but recovered to qualify for the World and China Opens. He couldn't halt the slide, however, and he missed out on the World Championships after losing in qualifying to Liu Chuang. He is currently ranked 27 in the world.

Name: Jamie Cope
Born: September 12th 1985, Stoke-on-Trent
Nationality: English
Turned Pro: 2002
Century Breaks: 105
Highest Break: 147
Ranking Titles: 0
World Titles: 0

Dale

Right: *Dominic Dale at the 2011 Paul Hunter Classic*

Dominic Dale won the 1991 Welsh Amateur Championships but then lost in the final of the World Amateur Championship. Despite this, he turned professional in 1992, but he didn't win his first ranking tournament, the Grand Prix, for another five years. He was only 57th in the world at the time and had to overcome John Higgins in the final.

His best performance in the World Championship came in 2000 when he beat Peter Ebdon and David Gray to reach the quarter-final, and he also reached the semi-final of the LG Cup (2002), the Northern Ireland Trophy (2006) and the Malta Cup (2008). Without ever reaching the top 16, he won his second ranking event at the 2007 Shanghai Masters. Despite being 6-2 down to Ryan Day, he rattled off eight consecutive frames to clinch the match.

He was solid again throughout 2010, 2011 and 2012, winning event six of the minor Players' Tour Championship, progressing to the quarter-final of the Australian Goldfields Open and beating Nigel Bond at the UK Championship. Dale was beaten by Judd Trump in the first round of the 2012 World Championship but still climbed the rankings to number 23.

He is one of the game's great characters and should challenge at all of the ranking events in 2013. He lost in the first round of the World Championship to semi-finalist Judd Trump, however.

Name: Dominic Dale
Born: December 29th 1971, Coventry
Nationality: Welsh
Turned Pro: 1992
Century Breaks: 109
Highest Break: 145
Ranking Titles: 2
World Titles: 0

Day

Above: *Ryan Day*

Ryan Day joined the professional UK tour in 1998, and he earned a young player award in 2000. He won the Benson & Hedges Championship the following year and qualified for the 2002 Masters, where he beat Dave Harold but eventually lost to Stephen Hendry. The next season he was beset with health problems and his form suffered but he was back to his best at the 2004 World Championship when he notched three centuries and led John Higgins 9-7 in the opening round. A missed pink cost him the match but Higgins had seen enough to know that Day would become a force in the game.

He reached the quarter-final of the 2005 Welsh Open and finished the year ranked 33 in the world. He enjoyed victory over Joe Perry at the Crucible in 2006 and almost beat Ronnie O'Sullivan in the second round but he faltered in the home stretch and went down 13-10. He scored a number of notable victories over Matthew Stevens, Ken Doherty and Mark Williams at the China Open, and he then defeated defending champion John Higgins at the 2008 World Championships, although Higgins had his revenge in the final of the Grand Prix. Day then lost to Matthew Stevens in the first round of the UK Championship.

Despite reaching number six in the world, his next two seasons were disappointing and he only reached one quarter-final (at the Welsh Open). His next highlight was a run to the quarter-final of the 2012 World Championship, although a migraine during his match with Matthew Stevens saw him lose 11 frames in succession and concede the match. He is currently just inside the world's top 32.

Name: Ryan Day
Born: March 23rd 1980, Bridgend
Nationality: Welsh
Turned Pro: 1998
Century Breaks: 162
Highest Break: 145
Ranking Titles: 0
World Titles: 0

Davis, Fred

Fred Davis initially devoted his supreme cueing skills to billiards and he won the Under-16 UK Championship in 1929. He immediately turned professional but the sport was in decline and he foresaw snooker overtaking it. He adapted to the subtle differences and first played in the World Snooker Championship in 1937, although he lost in the first round to Bill Withers. Fred's brother Joe exacted revenge in the next round by hammering Withers 30-1.

Fred put the defeat to Withers down to his poor eyesight so he had a pair of swivel-lens glasses made. He reached the semi-final in 1938 and 1939 before losing to Joe in the 1940 final 37-36, the only time that the brothers met in the deciding match. Joe retired from the World Championship after the war leaving Fred, who was 12 years his junior, to claim the 1948 title. He was the only player to beat Joe on level terms, which he managed four times.

Fred won the World Matchplay five times on the trot during the sport's golden age, but, despite filling large venues like the Blackpool Tower Circus, snooker soon lost its appeal and by the 1950s sometimes only four players would enter tournaments. Rex Williams revived the sport by re-introducing the World Championship on a challenge basis in 1964, but John Pulman dominated the event until the 1970s.

From 1969 the tournament changed format again, with the knockout rules familiar to us today being introduced. In the first quarter-final, Davis and Ray Reardon played an epic session that entered the Guinness Book of Records as the longest ever. Davis also finished runner up in the 1970 Pot Black competition, but he then suffered the first of two heart attacks and took time out to recuperate.

He was still a force throughout the late 1970s and recorded notable wins over Alex Higgins, John Spencer, Bill Werbeniuk and Patsy Fagan. In 1978 he proved he could still compete with the best when he beat John Virgo and Dennis Taylor on his way to the semi-final of the World Championship at the age of 64. He was a regular fixture at the Crucible until 1980

Left: *Fred Davis wins the 1948 World Championship*

but by then he was past his best and lost in the first round to David Taylor (he entered the qualifying tournament until 1984).

The following year Davis reached his last final, the Sheffield Shield, but he eventually lost to Terry Griffiths, the same player who had beaten him at his last Masters earlier in the season.

In June 1980 Davis joined his brother as the second player to win both the World Billiards and World Snooker titles. He maintained a high standard in the three-ball game until he was in his 80s. He retired from snooker in 1993 and died after a fall at home in 1998.

Name: Fred Davis, OBE
Born: August 14th 1913, Chesterfield
Died: April 16th 1998
Nationality: English
Turned Pro: 1929 - 1993
Highest Break: 142
Ranking Titles: 10
World Titles: 8

Davis, Joe

Below: *The incomparable Joe Davis won 15 world titles and retired in 1946 having never been beaten at the event*

Joe Davis must surely be a candidate for the greatest snooker player of all time. Like his brother, he began playing billiards at an early age and he won the Chesterfield Championship aged 13. He turned professional at 18 but lost his first world final to Tom Newman inv1926. He was runner up again the following year, but he exacted revenge over Newman in 1928 to claim his first title.

He defended the title for the next three years but lost the 1933 and 1934 finals to Australian Walter Lindrum. While he was at his peak he helped organise the first snooker World Championships in 1927. In an incredible run that has never been matched in snooker and hardly ever in any professional sport, Davis took the title every year until 1940, a year in which he beat younger brother Fred 37-36.

After the war, Joe took up where he'd left off and recorded his 15th consecutive win. He promptly retired as the only player to remain unbeaten in his entire World Championship career.

Although he no longer entered the World Championship, Davis was still the man to beat in the lesser tournaments. He won the News of the World event three times in the 1950s and then recorded the first official maximum break at an exhibition match in Leicester in 1955. (He'd also made the first century break in 1930.) He retired in 1964 but died two months after collapsing during his brother's epic World Championship semi-final against Perrie Mans in 1978.

Now that snooker's appeal is truly global and the standard is so high amongst the world's elite that they tend to share victories in the major events, Davis's records and unique achievements are unlikely to be matched.

Name: Joe Davis, OBE
Born: April 15th 1901, Derbyshire
Died: July 10th 1978, Hampshire
Nationality: English
Turned Pro: 1919 - 1964
Century Breaks: 687
Highest Break: 147
Ranking Titles: 22
World Titles: 15

Davis, Steve

Steve Davis learned to play snooker with his father, Bill, at the age of 12. He was a keen student of the Joe Davis method and the pair modelled Steve's technique and stance on the legendary pre-war player. He came to the attention of manager Barry Hearn through the Lucania chain of snooker halls, with Hearn then taking him round the country to play exhibitions against established stars like Ray Reardon and Alex Higgins.

Davis then won the English Under-19 billiards title in 1976, but he didn't turn pro as a snooker player for another two years. He first entered the World Championship in 1979 but he was beaten 13-11 by Dennis Taylor in the first round. The following year he beat defending champion Terry Griffiths on the way to the quarter-final and, although he eventually lost to Alex Higgins, the Steve Davis era had begun.

He won the UK Championship, the Classic, International Masters and English Professional titles, and was then tipped by bookmakers to take the world title in 1981 despite only being seeded 15th. Davis dominated the event and beat Doug Mountjoy 18-12 in the final.

In early 1982, Davis made snooker history by compiling the first televised 147 at the Classic in Oldham. Later that year he took the first of his three Masters titles. Although he succumbed to the Curse of the Crucible and failed to retain his world title, Davis then won the World Doubles Championship with partner Tony Meo and finally regained the world crown with an 18-6 demolition of Cliff Thorburn in the 1983 final. He won it again the following year with a narrow victory over the unfortunate Jimmy White.

Davis was again the hot favourite going into the 1985 tournament and he progressed easily to a final against Dennis Taylor. Davis produced a master-class in the first session and led 7-0, but Taylor fought back to 11-11 with some inspired snooker of his own. The pair traded frames going into the evening session but they couldn't be split and the match came down to a one-frame shootout. Taylor cleared the colours to the black but couldn't pot it and take the match so they traded safety shots and risky long pots before Davis over-cut a relatively straightforward shot to the corner

Above: *Steve Davis dominated snooker throughout the 1980s*

pocket. Amidst unbearable tension, Taylor composed himself and knocked it in for an 18-17 win. More than 18 million people watched the drama unfold and the moment was eventually voted the ninth greatest sporting moment in history in a 2002 poll.

Davis managed to put the disappointment behind him and took the 1985 Grand Prix and the UK Championship but he again came unstuck against an un-fancied opponent at the 1986 World Championship. Joe Johnson was a 150-1 outsider but he won convincingly and Davis's aura of invincibility seemed to be cracking. Davis responded to the setback by winning every major title in 1987: UK, Masters and World Championship. He took his sixth and last world title in 1989 with an 18-3 annihilation of John Parrott.

In the 1990s, Stephen Hendry became the sport's dominant force. Davis reached a number of world semi-finals but his last ranking tournament win was the 1995 Welsh Open. He then dropped out of the top 16 at the turn of the millennium and failed to qualify for the World Championships for two years. He contemplated retirement but felt he could still compete so he knuckled down and regained his place amongst the world's elite with solid performances at the 2004 Welsh Open (he lost the final to O'Sullivan having been in a winning position) and the 2005 World Championship (he lost to eventual winner Shaun Murphy in the quarter-final). At the UK Championship later that season, Davis reached his 100th career final.

His form then gradually declined, although he still produced the odd memorable display such as when he beat John Higgins – a 1-20 favourite – at the 2010 World Championships (during his record 30th appearance at the Crucible). Despite repeatedly being questioned about his future, Davis has not given any indication that he is ready to retire.

He is also a keen pool, chess and poker player, and he has written several books on snooker, chess and cookery.

Name: Steve Davis, OBE
Born: August 22nd 1957
Nationality: English
Turned Pro: 1978
Century Breaks: 325
Highest Break: 147
Ranking Titles: 28
World Titles: 6

Dennis

Tom Dennis was unlucky to be playing at the same time as the great Joe Davis. He reached the final of the World Championship four times (1927, 1929, 1930 and 1931) but he was beaten each time by the legend. At the 1931 event, the pair were the only entrants, and the match was played in a back room of Dennis's pub in Nottingham. He led Davis 14-10 and 19-16 but was eventually beaten 21-25. He made two more appearances at the finals but retired in 1933.

Name: Tom Dennis
Born: 1881
Died: 1939
Nationality: English
Turned Pro: 1927 - 1933
Ranking Titles: 0
World Titles: 0

Left: *The great Tom Dennis*

Doherty

Below: *Ken Doherty*

Ken Doherty started his career at Jason's club in Dublin with a warped cue, but he made an immediate impact on the professional circuit by reaching two semi-finals in the 1991/92 season. He then reached the final of the 1992 Grand Prix, although he narrowly lost to Jimmy White, 9-10. He joined the elite top 16 with victory at the 1993 Welsh Open, and he stayed there for the next 15 years.

Although his first few shots at the world title yielded little success, in 1997 he became only the third player from outside the UK to claim the title when he defeated Stephen Hendry 18-12. (Australian Horace Lindrum was the first overseas player to win the title in 1952, and Canadian Cliff Thorburn was the second in 1980.)

He reached two more world finals, in 1998 and 2003, but he lost the defence to John Higgins and the next final to Mark Williams. During the latter tournament, Doherty had to show all his grit and guile to mastermind unlikely comebacks against Graeme Dott, Shaun Murphy and Paul Hunter. He also fought back from 11-4 down to Williams in the final to level the match at 16-16, but he then missed an easy red that would have set him up for a straightforward clearance.

In 2000, Doherty became the first person to miss the last black of what would have been a 147 when he faltered in the final of the B&H Masters. Matthew Stevens rubbed salt in the wounds by then taking the match. Despite a number of setbacks and several poor performances, he ended the 2005/06 season ranked number two in the world, his highest position to date.

Doherty's performances in non-ranking events were still good but failures in the major tournaments saw him drop out of the top 16 in 2007/08. He then struggled for a couple of seasons before producing the first maximum of his career at the 2012 Paul Hunter Classic in Germany.

Doherty still uses his famous warped cue, although his dip in form means he is more often seen as a pundit with the BBC's commentary and analysis team.

Name: Ken Doherty
Born: September 17th 1958, Dublin
Nationality: Irish
Turned Pro: 1990
Century Breaks: 300
Highest Break: 147
Ranking Titles: 6
World Titles: 1

Donaldson

Walter Donaldson won the National Under-16 Billiards Championship in 1922 so he was obliged to turn professional immediately, but he didn't actually enter the World Snooker Championship until 1933. He lost in the semi-final to the great Joe Davis and repeated the feat in 1940.

When the tournament resumed after the war, Joe Davis won the 1946 event and promptly retired, leaving the way open for Donaldson to shine. He was the first Scot to take the professional snooker world title (1947), with wins over Horace Lindrum and Fred Davis, and he was one of the game's greatest long potters. He also compiled a world record 142 break.

From 1947 until 1954 he reached eight consecutive world finals but Donaldson could only beat Fred Davis once more, in 1950. With snooker in decline and his own form gradually deteriorating, he retired in 1954. He died at home in Buckinghamshire in 1973.

Left: *Walter Donaldson just before turning professional, 1922*

Name: Walter Donaldson
Born: January 4th 1907, Coatbridge
Died: May 26th 1973, Buckinghamshire
Nationality: Scottish
Turned Pro: 1923 - 1954
Highest Break: 142
Ranking Titles: 2
World Titles: 2

Dott

Below: *Graeme Dott celebrates winning the 2006 world title*

Graeme Dott won the UK Under-19 title in 1992 and the Scottish Amateur Championship in 1993, so he turned professional in 1994. He started steadily, reaching the quarter-final of the 1996 Welsh Open and the final of the 1999 Scottish Open. He gradually climbed the rankings and later that year he knocked in a 147 at the British Open.

In 2006, Dott realised his potential by winning the World Championship. En route to the final he beat John Parrott, Nigel Bond, Neil Robertson and Ronnie O'Sullivan. At nearly one o'clock in the morning, Dott finally overcame the challenge from Peter Ebdon and lifted the trophy. He continued his good form

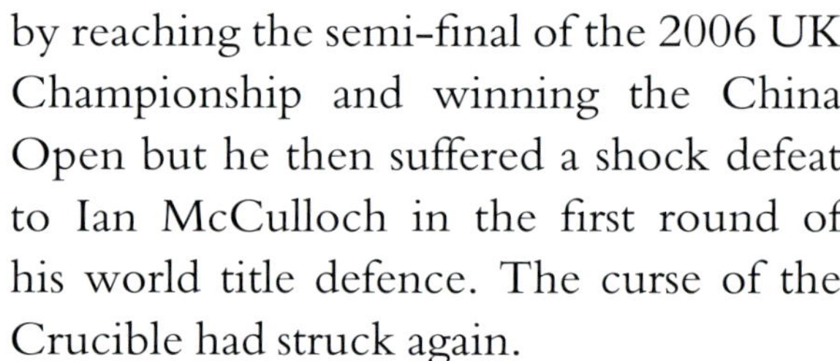

by reaching the semi-final of the 2006 UK Championship and winning the China Open but he then suffered a shock defeat to Ian McCulloch in the first round of his world title defence. The curse of the Crucible had struck again.

Despite a bright start to the 2007/08 season, Dott then lost 12 consecutive matches and announced that he might miss the World Championship as he was suffering from depression. He dropped down the rankings to number 28 but struggled on for two years before finally battling his way to the 2010 world final, although his spirited challenge was seen off by Neil Robertson. The following season he continued his return to form by making the world quarter-final, but then a number of poor results culminated in a 10-1 hammering at the hands of Joe Perry in the 2012 event. He then lost in the second round of the 2013 World Championship to Shaun Murphy.

Name: Graeme Dott
Born: May 12th 1977, Larkhall
Nationality: Scottish
Turned Pro: 1994
Century Breaks: 130
Highest Break: 147
Ranking Titles: 2
World Titles: 1

Drago

Tony Drago's rapid-fire all-action style has earned him the nickname 'Tornado'. He reached two major finals in an eventful career, although he was beaten at the 1991 World Masters by Jimmy White and by Stephen Hendry at the 1997 International Open. He climbed into the top 10 in the rankings on the back of these showings, and he eventually notched up 11 appearances at the Crucible. He also recorded a maximum break at the 2002 B&H Championship (he'd previously made a 149 in practice using a free ball, and he once made a century in three and half minutes).

He failed to qualify for the World Championship in 2004 and dropped out of the top 32. Four years later he dropped off the tour completely but he made a comeback the following season by qualifying for the Welsh Open and then the China Open. He broke back into the top 50 at the end of the 2011 season but he then won only four qualifying matches and again dropped down the rankings after losing to amateur Justin Astley.

Drago is also an accomplished pool player who won the 2003 World Masters and made it to the semi-final of the World Championship.

Above: *Having dropped off the main tour, Drago brought his considerable skills to the pool table*

Name: Tony Drago
Born: September 22nd 1965, Valletta
Nationality: Maltese
Turned Pro: 1985
Century Breaks: 119
Highest Break: 147
Ranking Titles: 0
World Titles: 0

Ebdon

Below: *Peter Ebdon pots a red in the centre pocket during the 2010 Brugge Open*

Sporting a ponytail, Peter Ebdon caused a stir soon after turning professional when he beat Steve Davis in the first round of the 1992 World Championship. He eventually reached the quarter-final but was knocked out by an in-form Terry Griffiths. He was awarded the Young Player of the Year on the back of these performances and he soon won his first ranking event, the 1993 Grand Prix.

He was solid for the next few seasons and reached a career-high of three in the world rankings after his run to the world final in 1996. Stephen Hendry was at the peak of his powers, however, and he beat Ebdon comfortably, 18-12. Ebdon's finest hour came at the 2002 World Championship (despite starting the tournament as a 33-1 outsider) when he exacted revenge over Hendry with the narrowest of wins.

Ebdon often attracts criticism for his methodical style of play, but there's no doubt that his gritty determination has seen him out of many a tight spot, particularly against Ronnie O'Sullivan at the 2005 World Championship when he came from 10-6 down to win 13-11. The following year he made the final again, but Graeme Dott edged the match 18-14. Ebdon recovered quickly, however, and he won the UK Championship by beating Hendry 10-6 in the final.

Apart from victory in the 2008 China Open, Ebdon's form had been patchy for a couple of years and he eventually dropped out of the top 16 in 2009 after 16 years amongst the elite. He returned to form in 2010/11 with a semi-final spot at the World Open and the quarter-final of the China Open, but he was eliminated early from the World and UK Championships.

A poor run of form was finally halted with a win at the 2012 China Open, and he also made the final of the Australian Goldfields Open, although he lost heavily to Barry Hawkins, 3-9.

Ebdon has been criticised for his exuberant celebrations and his occasional slow play, but he has apologised for both, claiming that neither is intentional. He is also colour blind and sometimes confuses the brown with a red.

Name: Peter Ebdon
Born: August 27th 1970, Islington
Nationality: English
Turned Pro: 1991
Century Breaks: 300
Highest Break: 147
Ranking Titles: 9
World Titles: 1

Ford

Tom Ford grew up playing the likes of Mark Selby and he was soon good enough to turn professional on the Challenge Tour. He didn't make much of an impact until he beat Ken Doherty at the 2005 Malta Cup, but he then lost to Stephen Hendry in the quarter-final. At the 2007 Grand Prix he made a 147 despite only just having been released from hospital.

He qualified for the 2010 World Championship by beating Judd Trump, but he then lost to Mark Allen in the first round. He won his first pro tournament – Event 3 of the Players' Tour Championship – the same year, and he then beat Tony Drago and Gerard Greene to make it to the last 32 of the UK Championship. Mark Allen again proved too strong, however, and he recorded a third straight win over Ford at the German Masters. Having reached the semi-final of the 2013 PTC he was ranked 26 in the world.

Above: *Tom Ford*

Name: Tom Ford
Born: August 17th 1983, Leicestershire
Nationality: English
Turned Pro: 2001
Century Breaks: 102
Highest Break: 147
Ranking Titles: 0
World Titles: 0

Foulds

Below: *Referee Jan Verhaas keeps a close eye on Neil Foulds at the 2011 World Seniors' Championship*

Far Right: *Peter Francisco*

Neal Foulds started playing aged 11 under the tutelage of father Geoff. He won the National Under-19 Championship and immediately turned professional. He qualified for the World Championship at his first attempt and proved it was no fluke by beating Alex Higgins in the first round. His run to the last 16 was ended by Doug Mountjoy but he still entered the rankings at number 30.

More strong performances, which included winning the BCE International Tournament in 1986, then finishing runner up to Steve Davis at the UK Championship and reaching the semi-final of the 1987 World Championship, saw him reach number three in the rankings. He also made the quarter-final of the 1988 World Championship, but then his form began to taper off.

He fought back in 1989/90 and maintained his place amongst the world's elite until 1993/94. He remained on the tour for another decade but he retired in 2004 to concentrate on a commentating career.

Name: Neal Foulds
Born: July 13th 1963
Nationality: English
Turned Pro: 1983 - 2004
Century Breaks: 76
Highest Break: 142
Ranking Titles: 1
World Titles: 0

Francisco, Peter

Peter Francisco was a talented South African who won the national championship seven times as an amateur and professional. He turned pro in 1984 and made it to the semi-final of the 1986 International Open and the 1987 Grand Prix, but it took until 1988 before he made the final stages of the World Championship in Sheffield.

He was a regular at the Crucible until 1995 when he lost a first-round match to Jimmy White, 10-2. There were unusual betting patterns on the game, however, and, having analysed the match, the World Snooker Association banned Francisco for five years because they believed he'd deliberately thrown the match.

Name: Peter Francisco
Born: February 13th 1962
Nationality: South African
Turned Pro: 1984 – 1995
Century Breaks: 18
Highest Break: 137
Ranking Titles: 0
World Titles: 0

Francisco, Silvino

Below: *Silvino Francisco*

Silvino Francisco is Peter's uncle. His brother Mannie is also a fine snooker and billiards player who was runner up in the World Amateur Billiards Championship. Silvino turned pro in 1978 but, despite reaching the quarter-final of the 1982 World Championship, he didn't make an impact until he beat Kirk Stevens 12-9 in the final of the 1985 British Open.

Despite winning, he accused Stevens of playing under the influence of banned substances, for which he was fined £6,000 and penalised ranking points. Stevens later admitted a drug problem, however, so the penalty was reversed.

Controversy dogged him throughout his career and he was also involved in a betting scandal when he lost 5-1 to Terry Griffiths in the 1989 Masters final. A large amount of money had been bet on that exact score and Francisco was arrested. He was released without charge but declared himself bankrupt in 1996 after gambling away his fortune. His career over, he was then arrested for smuggling cannabis and served three years in prison.

Name: Silvino Francisco
Born: May 3rd 1946
Nationality: South African
Turned Pro: 1978 – 1996
Century Breaks: 8
Highest Break: 128
Ranking Titles: 1
World Titles: 0

Fu

Marco Fu started playing snooker aged nine but he didn't take up the sport seriously until he'd emigrated to Canada with his parents when he was 12. In 1996, President of the Hong Kong Billiards Council Joseph Lo asked him to return home and turn professional. He initially declined but, having won the World Amateur and Under-21 titles, he turned pro and reached the final of the Grand Prix by beating Ronnie O'Sullivan and Peter Ebdon. He eventually lost to Steven Lee but Fu was now moving swiftly up the world rankings.

He made it to the Crucible in 1999 and was voted the sport's best newcomer, but then his form dipped and he struggled until enjoying a good run to the 2003 Welsh Open when he beat Lee and O'Sullivan on the way to the semi-final. Another run of poor performances saw him only just qualify for the 2003 World Championship but he overturned the odds by beating an in-form O'Sullivan in the first round. He then dispatched Alan McManus before eventually losing to Lee. He won his first title, the Invitational Premier League, with victory over Mark Williams.

Two below-par seasons saw him drop out of the top 32, but he then made the semi-final of the 2006 World Championship after beating McManus, Steven Maguire and Ken Doherty. He was 15-9 down to Peter Ebdon in the semi but he won seven of the next eight frames to send the match into a deciding frame, although Ebdon just edged him out.

Fu won the 2007 Grand Prix with victory over O'Sullivan, and more solid showings saw him climb back into the top 16. He then made the final of the 2008 UK Championship after a sensational fight-back against Ali Carter, but Shaun Murphy took the title in a tense but low-scoring final, 10-9. His next final wasn't until the 2010 Masters, but he then dropped out of the top 16. He began to claw back his ranking with a maximum at the 2012 World Open and a final appearance at the 2013 German Masters, although he eventually lost 6-9 to Ali Carter. He then reached the second round of the World Championship before losing to Judd Trump.

Name: Marco Fu
Born: January 8th 1978, Hong Kong
Nationality: Chinese
Turned Pro: 1998
Century Breaks: 227
Highest Break: 147
Ranking Titles: 1
World Titles: 0

Above: *Marco Fu plays a difficult shot with the spider at the Paul Hunter Classic*

Gould

Right: *Martin Gould signs an autograph at the 2012 Wembley Masters*

Martin Gould turned professional on the Challenge Tour in 2000, but he still won the English Amateur Championship in 2002. During qualifying for the 2003 World Championships he won eight matches against the likes of Alain Robidoux and Stephen Maguire. He eventually lost to Patrick Wallace and dropped off the tour, although he returned to claim a second amateur title in 2007.

Having returned to the tour he qualified for the 2008 UK Championship, although he narrowly lost to Shaun Murphy. He reached the last 16 of a ranking event for the first time at the 2009 Welsh Open, which included a victory over Stephen Hendry. At the 2010 World Championship he finally came of age, beating Marco Fu and then giving eventual champion Neil Robertson an almighty scare in one of the great Crucible matches. The Australian rallied from 7-0 down to level the scores at 12-12, and he then held his nerve to close out the match.

Gould repeated his first-round win over Fu in the 2011 World Championship, but he was then beaten by an in-form Judd Trump in the second round. By October, he had entered the elite top 16, and he then beat Ronnie O'Sullivan in the Power Snooker Masters final. In 2012 he won his first professional title at the second event of the PTC, and he backed it up by taking the Snooker Shootout title after overcoming Mark Allen in the one-frame event. The win netted him £32,000.

Name: Martin Gould
Born: September 14th 1981, Pinner
Nationality: English
Turned Pro: 2000
Century Breaks: 88
Highest Break: 139
Ranking Titles: 0
World Titles: 0

Gray

Above: *David Gray*

David Gray won the English Amateur title in 1995 and promptly turned professional, but it would be another two years before he recorded his first tour win, the non-ranking Benson & Hedges Championship. At the 2000 World Championships he caused one of the Crucible's greatest upsets when he beat Ronnie O'Sullivan 10-9 in the first round, this despite O'Sullivan knocking in five century breaks.

Gray played consistently well over the next two years and finally made his first ranking final at the 2002 Scottish Open having beaten Stephen Hendry, John Higgins and Peter Ebdon. Stephen Lee proved too strong in the final (9-2) but Gray was back the following year and he again knocked out Hendry and Higgins en route to the final. This time he overcame the challenge of Mark Selby and won his first ranking event, 9-7.

In 2004 he knocked in his first maximum and beat Selby and Joe Perry on his way to the final of the UK Championship and a career-high ranking of 12. He may have lost the final convincingly (10-1) against Stephen Maguire but he recovered to beat Jimmy White at the 2006 World Championship. He then gradually dropped down the rankings after poor performances at the Grand Prix and during qualifying for the 2007 World Championships. He failed to qualify for the professional tour from May 2011 to 2013.

Name: David Gray
Born: February 9th 1979, London
Nationality: English
Turned Pro: 1996
Century Breaks: 79
Highest Break: 147
Ranking Titles: 1
World Titles: 0

Griffiths

Below: *Dennis Taylor (left) and Terry Griffiths before their 1979 world final at the Crucible. Griffiths won the title at his first attempt*

Terry Griffiths had a number of jobs – postman, miner, bus conductor – before turning his attention to snooker and winning the 1975 Welsh Amateur Championship. He followed this up with the English amateur titles in 1977 and 1978 before he turned professional. His first pro match saw him race into a commanding 8-1 lead against the legendary Rex Williams at the UK Championships, but he then lost 9-8.

At the following year's World Championship he proved his talent by beating Perrie Mans, Alex Higgins and Eddie Charlton on his way to the final. He then defeated Dennis Taylor to become World Champion at the first attempt. He was also part of the Welsh team – with Ray Reardon and Doug Mountjoy – that won the inaugural World Cup, but he then suffered a shock loss to John Virgo in the final of the UK Championship.

He recovered to win the 1980 Masters against Alex Higgins in front of more than 2,000 people at the Wembley Conference Centre, but he then succumbed to the Crucible Curse by losing to Steve Davis in the first match of his world title defence. Griffiths and Davis met repeatedly in the finals of the next few events, with Davis winning all but two of the encounters, the 1982 Classic and the Irish Masters.

Griffiths didn't win another ranking title, although he did take the 1984 Malaysian Masters, the Singapore Masters, the 1985 Hong Kong Masters and the Belgian Classic. He returned to form in 1988 and made the final of the World Championship once more, but the 1980s were the Davis years and his old rival beat him convincingly, 18-11. Having lost again to Davis at the Crucible in 1996, he announced his retirement, although he did qualify for the 1997 World Championship.

Since his retirement Griffiths has gained wide praise as a coach and mentor to the likes of Marco Fu, Mark Williams, Ali Carter and Stephen Hendry. He also adds a little wit and wisdom to the BBC commentary team.

Name: Terry Griffiths, OBE
Born: October 16th 1947, Llanelli
Nationality: Welsh
Turned Pro: 1978 - 1997
Century Breaks: 75
Highest Break: 139
Ranking Titles: 1
World Titles: 1

Hallett

Mike Hallett was a solid player who never really hit the heights of contemporaries like Steve Davis and Jimmy White. He won the National Under-16 title 1975 but made little impact on the sport until the 1988 Masters when he secured four snookers in the semi-final against John Parrott to set up a final with Davis. He lost the match 9-0 but recovered to take the 1989 Hong Kong Masters (9-8) against Dene O'Kane.

Two years later he reached the Masters final for the second time. He raced to a 7-0 lead over Stephen Hendry. Needing just the pink and black in frame 11 to take the match, he missed and Hendry staged a remarkable comeback to win 9-8. Hallett returned home to find his house had been burgled – not a good day at the office.

He reached the quarter-final of the World Championship twice but his form gradually tapered off and he quit the main tour after a quarter of a century in 2005. He now works as an insightful commentator for Eurosport and Sky, and he also managed to beat Duane Jones on his way to meeting Ronnie O'Sullivan in the 2011/12 Players Tour Championship.

Above: *Mike Hallett*

Name: Mike Hallett
Born: July 6th 1959, Grimsby
Nationality: English
Turned Pro: 1980
Century Breaks: 48
Highest Break: 139
Ranking Titles: 1
World Titles: 0

Hamilton

Below: *Anthony Hamilton at the 2011 Paul Hunter Classic*

Anthony Hamilton had a quiet start to his professional career but he'd made his way into the top 32 by 1995. He then reached the final of the 1999 British Open and began the match with two centuries, but Fergal O'Brien pipped him to the title. He also reached the final of the 2001 China Open but narrowly lost to Mark Williams.

Despite being a prolific break-builder, Hamilton has never fared particularly well at the World Championships. He reached the quarter-final in 2000 but was demolished 13-3 by John Higgins. Eventual winner Peter Ebdon knocked him out at the same stage two years later (13-6), as did Ronnie O'Sullivan in 2004. He lost for the fourth time at the quarter-final stage in 2007 to Stephen Maguire.

The next season was poor and he failed to reach the last 16 in any of the ranking tournaments, and he also struggled in the minor events. However, he did make the semi-final of the 2009 Welsh Open by beating Peter Ebdon, Mark Selby and Michael Judge. He was leading Ali Carter in the semi but lost 5-6, and he then dropped out of the top 32. He rallied to reach the final of the Paul Hunter Classic in 2010 but he lost to Judd Trump and his ranking continued to slide.

Name: Anthony Hamilton
Born: June 29th 1971, Nottingham
Nationality: English
Turned Pro: 1991
Century Breaks: 218
Highest Break: 145
Ranking Titles: 0
World Titles: 0

Hann

Quinten Hann was the 1994 Under-21 World 8-Ball Pool Champion, but he then graduated towards snooker and turned professional in 1995. He made little impact on the sport, although he did manage a 143 break at the 1997 Grand Prix. He missed a number of tournaments after breaking his wrist motorbike racing in 1999 and, having then broken his foot after a parachute jump in 2000, he played barefoot at the UK Championship.

At the 2001 Grand Prix, Hann acquired his bad-boy image after repeatedly abusing the spectators and his opponent, the mild-mannered Anthony Hamilton. Hamilton won the match and then branded Hann a disgrace for his behaviour and for splitting the pack with pool-style break-off shots.

Three years later he was reprimanded for threatening fellow professional Andy Hicks with more obscene hand gestures and unsporting behaviour. Hicks retaliated by telling Hann that he was going to knock him out of the top 16, which he duly did. Hann then challenged Hicks to sort it out in the ring at a charity boxing match. Hicks declined so Mark King took up the challenge, although the volatile Australian won on points.

Hann then branded Gaelic footballers soft so another boxing match was arranged with Dublin GAA player Johnny Magge, with the latter winning in the three rounds. Before the first round of the 2005 World Championship, Hann went out drinking because his cue had been damaged. He was thrashed 10-2 the following day.

Above: *Australian Quinten Hann is one of snooker's bad boys*

Hann has also been in trouble away from the green baize: in 2002 he was tried but acquitted of rape, and he was cleared of two further sex attacks in 2005. The day after the second acquittal, The Sun newspaper produced evidence that Hann had agreed to lose a match against Ken Doherty at the China Open. He refused to attend the hearing and was found guilty in absentia. He was banned from snooker until 2014 and fined £10,000.

Name: Quinten Hann
Born: June 4th 1977
Nationality: Australian
Turned Pro: 1995 – 2006
Century Breaks: 39
Highest Break: 143
Ranking Titles: 0
World Titles: 0

Harold

Right: *Dave Harold*

When ranked only 93rd in the world, Dave Harold was the surprise winner of the 1993 Asian Open just two years after turning professional. In so doing, he became the lowest-ranked player ever to win a ranking tournament. He backed up this early promise by making the final of the 1994 Grand Prix, although he lost to John Higgins.

He made it into the top 16 in 1996 after reaching the semi-final of the Welsh Open and the quarter-final of the World Championship. His good form continued and he knocked out Stephen Hendry and John Higgins at the 1998 Grand Prix, although he lost in the semi-final to Stephen Lee. He lost again at the same stage the following year to Mark Williams.

A couple of poor seasons and a wrist injury saw him drop out of the top 16 but he came back strongly in 2008 and made it to the final of the Northern Ireland Trophy after wins over Graeme Dott, Stephen Lee, defending champion Stephen Maguire and John Higgins, although he couldn't upset Ronnie O'Sullivan in the final and lost 9-3. He hasn't managed to recapture this kind of form for a couple of years and has now dropped to 44 in the world.

Name: Dave Harold
Born: December 9th 1966, Stoke-on-Trent
Nationality: English
Turned Pro: 1991
Century Breaks: 126
Highest Break: 143
Ranking Titles: 1
World Titles: 0

Hawkins

Above: *Barry Hawkins*

Barry Hawkins was another slow starter in the professional ranks. It took him nine years to break into the world's top 32 after reaching the semi-final of the 2005 Welsh Open. He then reached the semi of the Grand Prix and the Welsh Open again the following season, and he also qualified for the World Championship for the first time. It was a baptism of fire, however. Ken Doherty thrashed him 10-1 in the opening round.

He appeared to be on the slide in the aftermath of the defeat and dropped out of the top 16, but he fought back to reach the last 16 at the 2007/08 Grand Prix, UK Championship and China Open. The following season he started strongly and won his first-round matches in four of the ranking events, which saw him re-enter the top 16. He continued to struggle at the Crucible, however, losing in the first round five times in a row. He finally ended his poor run with victory over Stephen Maguire in 2011 but he then narrowly lost 13-12 to Mark Allen in the second round.

The following season he won the shootout against Graeme Dott and collected £32,000, beat world number one Mark Selby at the Crucible, and then defeated Peter Ebdon in the final of the 2012 Australian Goldfields Open to claim his first ranking title. He then enjoyed a fantastic run at the 2013 World Championship, beating Jack Lisowski, world number one Mark Selby, Ding Junhui and Ricky Walden to secure a final spot against Ronnie O'Sullivan. Despite putting up a good fight against the Rocket, O'Sullivan was too good in every department and won 18-12. He has now jumped to number nine in the world rankings.

Name: Barry Hawkins
Born: April 23rd 1979, Dartford
Nationality: English
Turned Pro: 1996
Century Breaks: 141
Highest Break: 147
Ranking Titles: 1
World Titles: 0

Hendry

Stephen Hendry is one of four players in the modern era who, when at his best, has stood head and shoulders above his contemporaries, the other three being Steve Davis, John Higgins and Ronnie O'Sullivan. He started playing aged 12 when his father gave him a junior table and only two years later he won the Scottish Under-16 Championship. Having won the Scottish Amateur Championship and appeared on the BBC's Pot Black, Hendry turned professional.

He made an immediate impact by becoming the youngest Scottish Professional Champion and the youngest player to qualify for the World Championship, and then by winning the Grand Prix and the British Open. By the end of the 1987/88 season he was ranked four in the world. He continued his rise to superstardom by dominating the big events in 1989/90: he won the UK Championship, Dubai Classic, Asian Open, Scottish Open, Wembley Masters and then his first World Championship after a convincing 18-12 win over archrival Jimmy White.

He won a record five ranking titles the following year, although the Crucible Curse struck again when he lost to Steve James in the quarter-final of his world title defence. The following year he won the Grand Prix, the Masters and the Welsh Open, then rattled off ten frames on the bounce to defeat White for the world title. He rounded off the year with his first competitive maximum in the Matchroom League.

He then defended his world title twice, with the hapless Jimmy White missing an easy black to the corner during the 1994 final that would surely won him the match. Hendry promptly cleared up for an 18-17 win. The Hendry juggernaut rolled on and during the 1994 UK Championship final against Ken Doherty he knocked in seven centuries, playing what journalist David Hendon described as the best snooker ever seen.

In 1996 Hendry equalled the six world titles of Steve Davis and Ray Reardon, but Doherty then denied him a seventh with a comfortable 18-12 Crucible win in 1997. Hendry appeared to falter and he only won the Thailand Masters in the 1997/98 season. He also choked on a re-spotted black during the epic final of the 1998 Masters against Mark Williams and handed the Welshman the title. This convinced the establishment that Hendry was indeed a spent force but they were wrong. Form may be temporary but Hendry's class was permanent.

Despite losing his number one ranking for the first time in nearly a decade, then being dumped out of the 1998 World Championship in the first round by White, and also being thrashed 9-0 by un-seeded Marcus Campbell in the first round of the UK Championship, Hendry roared back by winning the Scottish Open and his seventh world crown.

He maintained his form by winning the British Open and knocking in his fifth competitive maximum, but he then inexplicably failed to win a ranking tournament in 2000/01 for the first time in 12 years. In 2002 he almost won his eighth world crown but he was beaten in the deciding frame by Peter Ebdon. He did claim the Welsh Open, British Open and Malta Cup in the next two seasons and so regained the coveted number one spot. But he couldn't reproduce the form of old and, despite reaching his 12th Crucible semi-final at the age of 39 in 2008, Hendry's career began to wind down.

He could still find the old magic occasionally, however. In 2012 he qualified for his 27th consecutive World Championship, and he knocked in his 11th maximum during his first-round match against Stuart Bingham. He then destroyed John Higgins 13-4 to reach his 19th quarter-final, although he was then soundly beaten by Stephen Maguire, after which he announced his retirement.

Hendry's records will be difficult to beat: amongst others, he has the most ranking titles, 36, and 72 tournament wins in all (second to Steve Davis); most consecutive wins at a single tournament; longest winning streak in ranking events; most years ranked number one (9), most century breaks (775); most prize money won (more than £8.5 million); and most competitive maximums (11, tied with O'Sullivan).

He now commentates for the BBC and runs a number of business ventures.

Above: *Stephen Hendry is the most successful player of the modern era*

Name: Stephen Hendry, MBE
Born: January 13th 1969, Edinburgh
Nationality: Scottish
Turned Pro: 1985 - 2012
Century Breaks: 775
Highest Break: 147
Ranking Titles: 36
World Titles: 7

Hicks

Below: *Andy Hicks*

Andy Hicks turned professional in the early 1990s but he didn't make waves until he reached the semi-final of the 1995 World Championship by beating Steve Davis, Willie Thorne and Peter Ebdon. The un-fancied Nigel Bond then blocked his march to the final. He also reached the semi-final of the 1996 Masters but he could never quite break into the world's top 16.

He looked like fading into obscurity when he rallied to reach the second round of the 2004 World Championship after an extraordinary first-round match against the volatile Australian Quinten Hann. Hann had repeatedly sledged him during the game so Hicks reminded the Aussie that he would be out of the top 16 if Hicks beat him. Hicks did prevail but the referee had to step in and separate them after the match. Hann challenged Hicks to a charity boxing bout so they could sort their differences out in the ring, but Hicks declined.

He enjoyed a brief upsurge in fortunes thereafter but by 2006/07 he was sliding back down the rankings. He did manage a 147 in the qualifying tournament for the 2012 UK Championship however.

Name: Andy Hicks
Born: August 10th 1973, Tavistock
Nationality: English
Turned Pro: 1991
Century Breaks: 134
Highest Break: 147
Ranking Titles: 0
World Titles: 0

Higgins, Alex

Alex 'Hurricane' Higgins was snooker's answer to George Best: brilliant, unpredictable and slave to the demons of drink and fame. He was born in Belfast and started playing snooker in his local club, the Jampot, aged 11. In 1963 the slightly built Higgins came to England for a career as a jockey but he couldn't keep to the weight after binging on Guinness and chocolate. He returned to Belfast and made his first (uncompetitive) maximum break. In 1968 he won the All-Ireland Amateur Snooker Championship and a new career beckoned.

He turned pro aged 22 and won his first world title at his first attempt by beating John Spencer in 1972. (He was the youngest winner until Stephen Hendry took the title aged 21 in 1990.) Higgins reached the final again in 1976 but, despite leading Ray Reardon 11-9, he capitulated and Reardon eventually won comfortably, 27-16. Higgins was runner-up again in 1980 to Cliff Thorburn despite building a commanding lead. He finally had his revenge over Reardon in 1982 when he won his second world title having knocked in a magnificent 135 in the final frame.

Higgins had always been a volatile player with an unusual action and he was frequently in the dock for his poor behaviour. But interspersed amongst the fights and bans he could compile the most memorable breaks. In the semi-final of the 1982 World Championship against Jimmy White he was on the verge of losing the match, but he then made a 69 clearance of such sublime skill and flair that it is frequently voted the best break of all time. He potted several impossible balls but could never quite get into prime position. Despite this, he eventually cleared the table and took the match.

He then produced another virtuoso display to come back from 7-0 down to beat Steve Davis 16-15 in the final of the 1983 UK Championship. He also won the Masters twice and another 14 minor titles. But Higgins's problems with drink and authority continued to dog him. He head-butted the referee at the 1986 UK

assaulting a referee at a charity match. By then he was seriously ill and he soon developed pneumonia. He also had cancerous growths removed from his throat.

In 2010 his friends tried to raise the £20,000 he needed for teeth implants because his had been destroyed by radiotherapy. He continued to drink and smoke excessively and was too ill to have the implants fitted, however. Towards the end of his life, Higgins was living in a caravan or sheltered housing and relying on state benefits having gambled his fortune away.

The 'Hurricane' may have been an inspiration to players like Jimmy White and Ronnie O'Sullivan but neither they nor fellow professionals like Ken Doherty and Steve Davis could save Higgins from himself and he died from a combination of malnutrition, pneumonia and cancer in July 2010.

Above: *Alex Higgins (left) was an erratic genius, Steve Davis his perfect foil*

Championship, for which he was fined and banned for five tournaments, then, having lost his first-round match at the 1990 World Championship, he punched official Colin Randle and threatened to have Dennis Taylor shot. He was then convicted of assaulting a 14-year-old boy, and was stabbed by his girlfriend.

He retired from the sport and spent his time playing for small sums of money in Northern Ireland, although he did receive invitations to play in the Irish Professional Championship in 2005 and 2006. The following year he was again accused of

Name: Alex Higgins
Born: March 18th 1949, Belfast
Died: July 24th 2010, Belfast
Nationality: Northern Irish
Turned Pro: 1971 - 1997
Century Breaks: 46
Highest Break: 142
Ranking Titles: 1
World Titles: 2

Higgins, John

John Higgins was a prodigiously talented youngster and he turned professional in 1992. Two years later he became the first teenager to win three ranking events in a season, and by 1996 he had climbed into the world's top 16. Since that time he has never dropped below number seven in the rankings and is one of the most consistent players the sport has known.

He narrowly lost the 1996 UK Championship to Stephen Hendry but he roared back with 14 centuries during the 1998 World Championship and took the title after an 18-12 demolition of defending champion Ken Doherty in the final. He then claimed the number one spot from Hendry, ending his compatriot's eight-year stay at the top. He also won the UK Championship and the Masters to become only the third player – after Davis and Hendry – to hold the three major titles at the same time. (Mark Williams became the fourth player to achieve this in 2003.) He also won the 1999 Grand Prix and the 2000 UK Championship. He reached the world final in 2001 but lost to an inspired Ronnie O'Sullivan, but he then became the first player to win the first three events of a snooker season when he took the Champions' Cup, Scottish Masters and British Open.

In the final of the 2005 Grand Prix, Higgins proved himself one of the game's elite when he became the first person to knock in four consecutive centuries in a ranking tournament. He then beat O'Sullivan again to win the 2006 Masters.

He lost the number one ranking to Mark Williams and Ronnie O'Sullivan but finally regained it after winning his second world title in 2007 when he overcame Mark Selby at the Crucible. He delivered his third World Championship in 2009 with a storming 18-9 win over Shaun Murphy. Having again regained the top spot, Higgins was caught out by a tabloid sting in which he appeared to agree to lose frames in four tournaments and discussed how to fix frames and matches.

Higgins denied the charges and claimed that he had feared for his safety (the sting took place in Kiev and he believed the Russian

Right: *John Higgins is one of today's greatest players*

Mafia might be involved) so he simply went along with the proposal with no intention of breaching the rules. An investigation by the WPBSA's disciplinary committee eventually withdrew the match-fixing charges but found him guilty of giving the impression that he would breach gambling rules and of failing to report the illegal approach by the News of the World. He received a six-month ban and was fined £75,000.

Higgins returned and proved he'd lost none of his appetite for the game by winning the European Players Tour Championship, the Prague Classic and the UK Championship. He regained the world number one spot with several non-ranking victories and then his fourth World Championship in 2011 after an epic final against Judd Trump. His defence of the title was poor, however, and he was thrashed by Hendry in the second round. He is currently ranked seventh in the world, although he suffered a surprise defeat to Mark Davis in the first round of the 2013 World Championship.

Name: John Higgins, MBE
Born: May 18th 1975, Wishaw
Nationality: Scottish
Turned Pro: 1992
Century Breaks: 510
Highest Break: 147
Ranking Titles: 25
World Titles: 4

Higginson

Andrew Higginson would probably have faded into obscurity had it not been for a remarkable performance at the 2007 Welsh Open. He'd made little impact as a professional and had only flirted with the main tour after a few seasons on the Challenge Tour. He then surprised everyone by beating Steve Davis and reaching the last 16 at the 2007 Malta Cup.

Higginson then hit an extraordinary run of form at the Welsh Open. He demolished Ali Carter 5-1 in a match which included his first professional maximum break, then rattled off five frames on the bounce to defeat John Higgins. He also beat Michael Judge and Stephen Maguire on his way to the final, the first unranked player to reach a ranking final since Terry Griffiths won the 1979 World Championship. He was 2-6 down to Neil Robertson at the end of the first session but he then staged a remarkable comeback and took six frames on the spin to lead 8-6. Robertson recovered to take the match to a deciding frame, however, which the Australian eventually won.

It had been a good week for Higginson though. He pocketed £17,500 as the runner-up but also received a cheque for £22,000 for his 147. A couple of quiet seasons were followed by his first visit to the Crucible in 2009, although he lost a tight opening match to Shaun Murphy. He won the PTC Event 5 by beating World Champion John Higgins and promptly qualified for several ranking events. He is currently ranked 22 in the world.

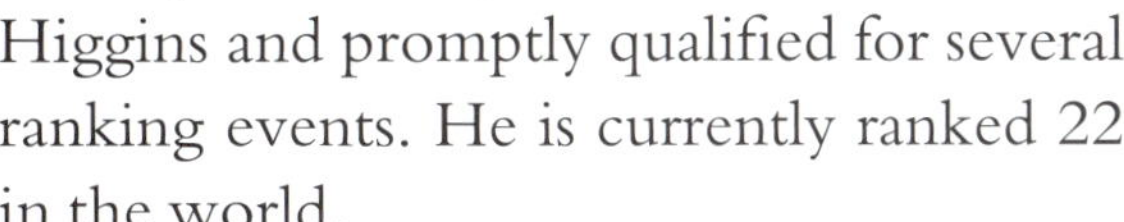

Above: *Andrew Higginson*

Name: Andrew Higginson
Born: December 13th 1977, Cheshire
Nationality: English
Turned Pro: 1995
Century Breaks: 88
Highest Break: 147
Ranking Titles: 0
World Titles: 0

Holt

Right: *Michael Holt*

Michael Holt was another player who seemed destined for obscurity but he eventually made a name for himself at the 2005 World Championship when he beat sparring partner Paul Hunter in the first round. In the second round he was thrashing Steve Davis (8-2) only for the six-time champion to stage a remarkable recovery and win 13-10. He lost in the first round to Peter Ebdon the following year but then won the non-ranking German Open. He also beat Ronnie O'Sullivan in the 2007 Malta Cup, although he lost in the next round to Mark King. He dropped out of the world's top 32 after failing to reach the last 16 of a ranking event in 2008.

Despite improving in 2009, a year in which he reached the Crucible after tough qualifying matches against Mark Davis and Dominic Dale, Holt has been criticised for his volatile temperament. He has been docked frames for swearing and once conceded a match in the deciding frame when there were still 13 reds on the table. He smacked the table so hard in anger that he broke a knuckle. Several solid performances in late 2012 and early 2013 have seen him climb back into the world's top 32.

Name: Michael Holt
Born: August 7th 1978, Nottingham
Nationality: English
Turned Pro: 1996
Century Breaks: 117
Highest Break: 145
Ranking Titles: 0
World Titles: 0

Hunter

Paul Hunter spent many hours on the practice table as a youngster and he was occasionally mentored by Joe Johnson. Aged 12 he was tipped for greatness, and he delivered in 1992 when he won the English Junior Doubles title with Richard Brooke. He turned professional three years later and promptly beat Alan McManus to reach the second round of the UK Championship. Aged just 17, he then became the youngest person to reach the last four of a ranking event (1996 Welsh Open).

Despite continuing in a good vein of form, he was fined and docked ranking points after testing positive for cannabis in 1997, but he bounced back by winning the 1998 Welsh Open after victories over Steve Davis, Nigel Bond, Alan McManus, Peter Ebdon and John Higgins. Having reached the semi-final of the 1998 UK Championship he was voted Young Player of the Year.

He reached number 12 in the rankings after his first Crucible appearance in 1999, although he lost narrowly to eventual champion Stephen Hendry. In the 2001 Masters Hunter admitted to having sex with his girlfriend during the interval. He was being thrashed by Fergal O'Brien in the final but came back to the table and rattled off four centuries in six frames to clinch the title. He defended it the following year and enjoyed a number of other tournament successes, notably at the 2002 British Open and the Welsh Open.

Ken Doherty knocked him out of the 2003 World Championship in the semi-final, but he roared back to claim his third Masters in four years with a tight victory over Ronnie O'Sullivan in the deciding frame. He began the 2004/05 season well by reaching the semi-final of the Grand Prix and the quarter-final of the China Open, but he then revealed that he'd been diagnosed with malignant neuroendocrine tumours, an aggressive form of cancer.

Hunter's form dipped during his treatment and he lost 5-10 against Neil Robertson in his last match, the first round of the 2006 World Championship. Hunter succumbed to the disease in October 2006. Despite many fellow professionals calling for the Masters to be renamed in his honour, the minor-ranking German Open is now known as the Paul Hunter Classic instead. He was posthumously awarded the BBC's Sports Personality of the Year Helen Rollason Award in December 2006. The Paul Hunter Foundation now gives disadvantaged children opportunities to play sport.

Name: Paul Hunter
Born: October 14th 1978, Leeds
Died: October 9th 2006, Huddersfield
Nationality: English
Turned Pro: 1995 - 2006
Century Breaks: 114
Highest Break: 146
Ranking Titles: 3
World Titles: 0

James

Steve James made little impact on the snooker scene until 1990. At the World Championships in Sheffield he was awarded a free ball after Alex Higgins had fouled and James used a colour as an extra red. He then cleared the table for the first 16-red total clearance in tournament history. He also beat Warren King to take the Mercantile Credit Classic.

The following year he beat Stephen Hendry to reach the semi-final of the World Championship but he was then beaten by Jimmy White. He declared himself bankrupt in 1998 having blown the £700,000 he'd earned from the sport.

Name: Steve James
Born: May 2nd 1961, Cannock
Nationality: English
Turned Pro: 1986
Century Breaks: 70
Highest Break: 142
Ranking Titles: 1
World Titles: 0

Left: *Steve James*

Far Left: *Paul Hunter lifted the Masters trophy three times during his short career*

Johnson

Below: *Joe Johnson was the surprise 1986 World Champion*

Far Right: *Tony Jones with the 1991 European Open trophy*

Joe Johnson reached the final of the World Amateur Championships in 1978 and turned professional immediately. He had to wait four years before reaching the final of the 1983 Professional Players' Tournament, although he was beaten by Tony Knowles, 9-8. Three years later he qualified for the Crucible having never won a match at the World Championships. He proved his doubters and the bookmakers wrong – they had him as a 150-1 outsider for the title – by beating Terry Griffiths and Knowles to set up a final against the all-conquering Steve Davis.

He overturned the odds and beat Davis convincingly (18-12) but he had a poor season as World Champion and only reached one semi-final. He wasn't tipped to repeat his success at the 1987 tournament but he defended the title valiantly and again made the final, although Davis exacted revenge and won 18-14. Johnson then won the Scottish Masters and reached the semi-final of the UK Championship after missing the pink in a maximum attempt.

He couldn't maintain his form and made his final Crucible appearance in 1991 before dropping out of the top 32 by the middle of the decade. Despite heart and eye problems, Johnson won the 1997 Senior Pot Black title. He was also a big influence on Paul Hunter during the latter's early career. He now runs two coaching academies, commentates for Eurosport and is known as the man who came closest to overcoming the famous Crucible Curse (no first-time champion has ever defended the world title at the venue) by reaching the final the following year.

Name: Joe Johnson
Born: July 29th 1952, Bradford
Nationality: English
Turned Pro: 1979 - 2004
Century Breaks: 46
Highest Break: 141
Ranking Titles: 1
World Titles: 1

Jones

Tony Jones seemed destined for greatness when he won the 1983 English Amateur Championship after defeating John Parrott in the final. He turned professional the following year and was runner-up with doubles partner Ray Reardon at the World Championships in 1985. He hovered around the top 32 for the next five years and was the surprise winner of the 1991 European Open. He entered the top 16 on the back of this but he never regained the heights and gradually slipped back down the rankings.

Name: Tony Jones
Born: April 15th 1960, Nottinghamshire
Nationality: English
Turned Pro: 1984
Century Breaks: 33
Highest Break: 135
Ranking Titles: 1
World Titles: 0

Judge

Below: *Michael Judge at the 2001 World Championship*

Having joined the pro ranks in 1991, Michael Judge made little impact for six years, but he then reached the quarter-final of the 1997 British Open. Four years later he knocked Jimmy White out of the World Championships at the 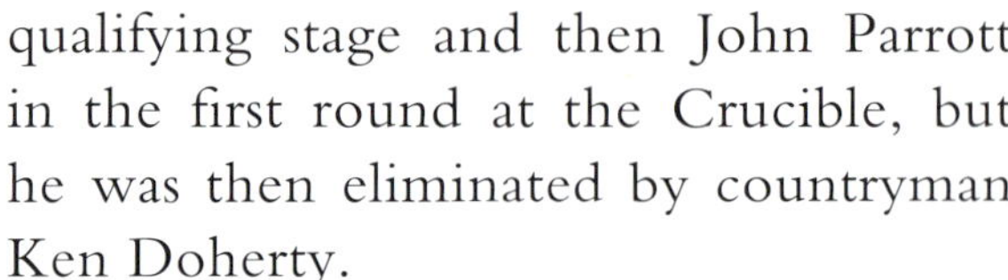 qualifying stage and then John Parrott in the first round at the Crucible, but he was then eliminated by countryman Ken Doherty.

Peter Ebdon knocked him out in the first round the following year but he then beat Mark Williams to reach the semi-final of the 2004 Grand Prix. He also knocked in a career-best 144 at that year's European Open. His form continued to improve in 2006/07 and he climbed to number 34 in the world after a run to the last 16 at the Welsh Open. The following year he enjoyed victories over Nigel Bond and Graeme Dott, but he eventually retired after a poor showing at the 2010 Welsh Open.

Name: Michael Judge
Born: January 12th 1975, Dublin
Nationality: Irish
Turned Pro: 1991 – 2011
Century Breaks: 62
Highest Break: 144
Ranking Titles: 0
World Titles: 0

Junhui

Ding Junhui's father took him to a snooker centre in Shanghai at the age of nine and, when he realised his son was going to be a star, he sold his house so that Ding could forge a career in the sport. In 2002 Ding won the Asian Under-21 Championship and then became the youngest winner of the Under-21 World Championship (15). He turned professional the following year and was soon ranked the top player in China.

In early 2004 he was awarded a wildcard to the Masters. He beat Joe Perry in the first round but lost narrowly to Stephen Lee. He then beat Peter Ebdon, Marco Fu and Ken Doherty en route to the final of the 2005 China Open. He took the title with a convincing win over Stephen Hendry while a record TV audience of 110 million tuned in. In December he beat Steve Davis in the final of the UK Championship, the first time the title had been won by a player from outside the British Isles. He then secured his third ranking title with a 9-6 victory over Ronnie O'Sullivan at the Northern Ireland Trophy.

In 2007 he made a maximum at the Masters (the first since Kirk Stevens in 1984) but he was out of sorts in the final and lost to O'Sullivan. A poor run of form saw him knocked out in the first round of the World Championship. By 2009 he was back to his best and he claimed his second UK Championship with victory over Mike Dunn, Shaun Murphy, Ali Carter, Stephen Maguire, and then John Higgins in the final (10-8). He won his first Masters two years later with victory over Marco Fu in the final. He then reached the semi-final of the 2011 World Championship but he couldn't squeeze past Judd Trump and eventually lost 15-17. The following season was quiet by comparison, although he did win the Welsh Open. He reached the quarter-final of the 2013 World Champion but was beaten by surprise runner-up Barry Hawkins.

Ding has now compiled more than 200 century breaks with five maximums, and he continues to be an inspiration for millions of his countrymen who are threatening to dominate the sport for the next generation.

Above: *Ding Junhui is one of the game's brightest prospects*

Name: Ding Junhui
Born: April 1st 1987, Jiangsu
Nationality: Chinese
Turned Pro: 2003
Century Breaks: 227
Highest Break: 147
Ranking Titles: 6
World Titles: 0

King

Below: *Mark King at the 2011 Paul Hunter Classic*

Mark King was a keen amateur and he turned professional in 1991. He didn't make much of an impact until reaching the final of the 1997 Welsh Open, which propelled him into the top 32. He continued his progress and remained in the top 16 for much of the next decade. At the 2004 World Championship he took up Quinten Hann's challenge, which had been to Andy Hicks, to sort out their differences in the boxing ring, but Hann won the bout on points.

Back on the baize, King beat Mark Williams, Alan McManus and John Parrott en route to the semi-final of the 2004 UK Championship, although he eventually lost to Stephen Maguire (9-4). King consistently reached the quarter-finals of the major events but he never seemed to be able to push on and win ranking tournaments. This was reflected in his world ranking which hovered between 16 and 32 for much of the latter half of the decade.

He then reached the semi-final of the Shanghai Masters in 2011 and followed this up with a quarter-final berth at the World Open but he was beaten by Mark Selby and Mark Allen respectively. He gained revenge over Mark Allen by knocking him out in the first round of the 2013 World Championship, although King was then beaten by Ding Junhui.

King is usually a fluent break-builder when amongst the balls but he occasionally loses control of the white when under pressure. His tactical nous and determination have been enough to see him reach the latter stages of tournaments but he is sometimes criticised for being too negative.

Name: Mark King
Born: March 28th 1974, London
Nationality: English
Turned Pro: 1991
Century Breaks: 95
Highest Break: 146
Ranking Titles: 0
World Titles: 0

Knowles

Tony Knowles started playing against his brothers aged nine in a social club run by his father. He was a keen student of the game and won the UK Junior Championship in 1972 and again two years later. He tried to turn professional shortly afterwards but the WPBSA refused him twice. When he threatened legal action, he was finally accepted into the pro ranks.

In 1982 Knowles stunned the snooker establishment by cruising to a comfortable 10-1 win over defending World Champion Steve Davis in the first round of the tournament. He backed this up with wins at the Jameson International and the 1983 Professional Players' Tournament. He then reached the semi-final of the 1983 World Championships and was leading Cliff Thorburn 15-13 before the Canadian fought back to win by a single frame. He cemented his place amongst the elite by making the semi-final again in 1985 and 1986 but by the early 1990s he was past his best and he dropped off the main tour in 1997.

Left: *Tony Knowles shares a joke with the crowd*

He was elected to a director's role by World Snooker early in the new millennium and he still enters the qualifying events for the World Championship. In 2009 he won the inaugural Super 6 tournament at the Crucible.

Name: Tony Knowles
Born: June 13th 1955, Bolton
Nationality: English
Turned Pro: 1980 - 1997
Century Breaks: 46
Highest Break: 139
Ranking Titles: 2
World Titles: 0

Lawler

Below: *Rod Lawler*

Rod Lawler reached the last 32 of the Dubai Classic in his first professional season but he then remained relatively quiet until he made it to the final of the 1996 International Open after a notable 5-3 win over Stephen Hendry. He lost in the final to John Higgins but then reached his second final at the 1994 Benson & Hedges Championship, although he lost to Mark Williams.

The following year he continued his good form by reaching the semi-final of the Malta Masters but he lost to home favourite, the 'Tornado' Tony Drago. He then qualified for the World Championships but lost in the last 32 to Peter Ebdon. In 1996 he made it to the Crucible again by beating Dennis Taylor in qualifying but, despite then beating John Parrott, he lost to Dave Harold in the last 16 of the tournament proper.

He had a lean period between making the last 16 of the 1998 UK Championship and the last 32 of the 2009 China Open, during which he only made the quarter-final of the 2003 Welsh Open. In 2011/12 he dropped to 73 in the world and his career looked to be over, but he fought back to regain his place on the tour and qualify for the 2012/13 Wuxi Classic. He beat Li Hang and Stephen Maguire but narrowly lost to Graeme Dott in the last 16. He then won his first professional title, the Players Championship Event 3, and moved back into the top 64.

Name: Rod Lawler
Born: July 12th 1971, Liverpool
Nationality: English
Turned Pro: 1990
Century Breaks: 72
Highest Break: 143
Ranking Titles: 0
World Titles: 0

Lawrence

Fred Lawrence was a prodigiously talented billiards player who once scored a break of 1,864. He reached the quarter-final of the 1927 World Snooker Championship but was beaten 8-7 by Tom Dennis. The following year he made the final but he couldn't overcome the great Joe Davis and went down 13-16. In 1929 and 1930 he again reached the semi-finals but again Joe Davis proved his nemesis, 13-10 and 13-2. He returned to the event after the war but he couldn't qualify for the finals and retired in 1947.

Name: Fred Lawrence
Born: 1895, Birmingham
Nationality: English
Turned Pro: 1927 - 1947
Ranking Titles: 0
World Titles: 0

Left: *Fred Lawrence*

Lee

Right: *Stephen Lee uses the rest to take on a difficult long pot at the 2011 Paul Hunter Classic*

Stephen Lee won the English Amateur Championship in 1992 and immediately turned professional. In his first season he won a world record 33 consecutive frames in qualifying tournaments but it still took him five years to break into the top 16. His smooth and stylish cue action has been rated the best in the game and he used it effectively to win his first ranking title, the 1998 Grand Prix, with hard-fought victories over Dave Harold and Marco Fu.

He failed a drug test in 2000 but was soon back to his best and he scored more ranking points than any other player in 2001/02 by winning the Scottish Open and the Grand Prix. He made the semi-final of the 2003 World Championship but his form then dipped and he failed to make an impression until the 2006 Welsh Open, which he won against World Champion Shaun Murphy despite being outside the world's elite.

He reached the final of the 2008 Masters but then considered retirement after a poor World Championship. His erratic form led to his arrest on suspicion of cheating in 2010 and he was dumped out of the subsequent UK and World Championships by eventual winner John Higgins.

He bounced back with a semi-final berth at the German Masters, a quarter-final of the Welsh Open, and then a final appearance at the World Open (he lost 10-1 to Mark Allen). His continuing good form saw him re-enter the top 16 at number eight, his highest ranking for a decade.

Despite this, Lee is still being investigated for alleged match-fixing. His appeal against a suspension in October 2012 was unsuccessful and his case will now be heard by Sport Resolutions UK.

Name: Stephen Lee
Born: October 12th 1974, Trowbridge
Nationality: English
Turned Pro: 1992
Century Breaks: 160
Highest Break: 145
Ranking Titles: 5
World Titles: 0

Lindrum

Horace Lindrum was born in Australia into a family of cue-sport enthusiasts: his great-grandfather was the first national billiards champion and his grandfather was noted coach William Lindrum. He made his first century at the age of 16 and then recorded a 1,431 break at billiards. Three years later he won the Australian Professional Billiards Championship, and he then took the snooker equivalent at the age of 22. He retained both titles for the next three decades, a unique sporting achievement.

Lindrum was unlucky to be competing at the same time as the legendary Joe Davis and he came second to the Englishman five times in the World Professional Snooker Championship. He finally won the title in 1952 (after Davis had retired) when he beat billiards champion Clark McConachy 94-49 after a mammoth 143-frame match. This two-week marathon was the highlight of his career, although several professionals had boycotted the event so they could play in the World Matchplay competition instead. Lindrum's victory was the last by an Australian until Neil Robertson took the world title in 2010.

His book, Snooker, Billiards & Pool, was an international bestseller between 1948 and 1974, and his records still hold up today. He made two world-record breaks in 1936: 135 and then 141; he is the only player to have held 11 national championships simultaneously (including the English, African, Chinese, Indian and Australian); he and Willie Smith were the first to play on television (at the Alexandra Palace); and he was the first player to make more than 1000 century breaks during public performances. For these remarkable achievements, he is rightly considered as one of the game's greatest players.

Above: *Horace Lindrum attempts a difficult swerve*

Name: Horace Lindrum
Born: January 15th 1912, Sydney
Died: June 20th 1974, Sydney
Nationality: Australian
Turned Pro: 1931 - 1964
Century Breaks: 1,000+
Highest Break: 143
Ranking Titles: 0
World Titles: 1

Lisowski

Below: *Jack Lisowski has battled cancer to reach the pinnacle of the game*

Jack Lisowski came second at the 2007 Junior Pot Black tournament and was awarded the Paul Hunter Scholarship – he had been diagnosed with Hodgkin's Lymphoma – which gave him the chance to practice with and play against the professionals. He responded well to treatment and won two events of the International Open Series, giving him a place on the main tour.

He struggled initially but then won five matches to reach the semi-final of the PTC's Event 6. He squeezed past Mark Selby (4-3) but was then beaten in the final by Tom Ford (0-4). He played well throughout 2011/12 and finished 24th in the order of merit. He also qualified for the Shanghai Masters, and almost won Event 1 of the 2012 PTC but he missed the yellow and handed victory to Stephen Maguire.

In his third qualifying match for the 2012 UK Championship he made his first maximum, and he then cemented his place among the world's elite by qualifying for the 2013 World Championships. He is another young player who was tipped to cause an upset at the season's main event in Sheffield but he was comprehensively outplayed by Barry Hawkins in the first round.

Name: Jack Lisowski
Born: June 25th 1991, Cheltenham
Nationality: English
Turned Pro: 2010
Century Breaks: 37
Highest Break: 147
Ranking Titles: 0
World Titles: 0

Maguire

Stephen Maguire joined the professional ranks on the UK tour in 1998 and he almost qualified for the World Championship in 2000 when he ran Joe Swail close in the qualifying event. He finally made an impact when he defeated Stephen Lee in the opening match of the 2002 UK Championship. He backed this up by winning the 2004 European Open against Jimmy White while only ranked 41 in the world. He then qualified for the World Championships proper for the first time, although he lost his first-round match to Ronnie O'Sullivan.

In 2004/05 Maguire cemented his reputation as one of the game's brightest talents. He reached the quarter-final of the Grand Prix, then demolished O'Sullivan in the semi-final of the British Open (6-1), only to lose to John Higgins in the final. He continued his good run by claiming his first title at the UK Championship, beating Mark King, Mark Davis, Stephen Lee, Ronnie O'Sullivan and Steve Davis on his way to the final where he destroyed David Gray 10-1.

He then had a couple of quiet seasons before blazing back to reach the semi-final of the 2007 World Championship. He was leading John Higgins 14-10 but couldn't close out the match and Higgins recovered to win 17-15. He did make the final of the UK Championship but O'Sullivan blew him away 10-2. He then compiled his first maximum at the 2008 China Open on his way to victory in the tournament.

He failed to win a ranking event the following season but reached the semi-finals in Shanghai and the UK Championships, which was enough to preserve his world number two spot. The following season he too found himself in trouble with the authorities and he was formally detained after allegations that he and Jamie Burnett had deliberately fixed their match at the 2008 UK Championship. These allegations are extremely difficult to prove and Maguire has dismissed them out of hand.

He promptly won the 2009 Grand Prix and reached the latter stages of the UK Championship, the 2010 Masters and the semi-final of the Welsh Open. He was beaten in the final of the Welsh Open by John Higgins the following year and he started 2011/12 poorly with more defeats at the Shanghai Masters and the UK Championship. His season picked up, however, and he breezed into the world semi-final after wins over Luca Brecel, Joe Perry and Stephen Hendry, but he finally came unstuck against Ali Carter. He finished the season ranked fourth and started the 2012/13 season strongly with victory at the Welsh Open over Stuart Bingham.

Name: Stephen Maguire
Born: March 13th 1981, Glasgow
Nationality: Scottish
Turned Pro: 1998
Century Breaks: 250
Highest Break: 147
Ranking Titles: 5
World Titles: 0

Mans

Perrie Mans won the national amateur tournament at his first attempt in 1960 and turned professional immediately. He then beat Freddie van Rensberg to claim the South African Professional Championship, the first of his 23 national titles, in 1965. He entered his first World Championship in 1970 but he couldn't win a match at the event until 1973 when he beat Ron Gross. The following year he caused a major upset by beating John Spencer in the second round but he was then thumped 15-4 by Rex Williams in the quarter-final.

He continued to improve and reached the semi-final the following year, although he then lost to defending champion Ray Reardon. In 1977 he won the first Pot Black tournament. He was back at the Crucible in 1978 but he lost a thrilling final 25-18 to Reardon having already beaten Spencer, Graham Miles and Fred Davis. His performances saw him reach the number two spot in the world rankings.

He won the Heidelberg 100 invitation event, then the 1979 Benson & Hedges Masters. He backed this up with a surprise win over Steve Davis at the 1981 Masters, but his career then slowly declined and he last played at the World Championships in 1986. He retired in 1987 but continued to play on the Senior Tour until 2000.

Left: *Perrie Mans eyes up a long pot*

Far Left: *Stephen Maguire at the 2012 German Masters*

Name: Perrie Mans
Born: October 14th 1940
Nationality: South African
Turned Pro: 1961 - 1987
Ranking Titles: 0
World Titles: 0

McConachy

Right: *Clark McConachy*

Clark McConachy was an outstanding cueist whose longevity in a sport is almost without equal. He was New Zealand Professional Billiards Champion for an astonishing 66 years and was World Champion for 17 years (1951 to 1968) until he was finally beaten by Rex Williams.

The strict teetotaller and advocate of physical fitness kept himself in excellent condition and reached the final of the World Snooker Championship in 1932 – when he lost to Joe Davis – and 1952, when he was beaten by Australian Horace Lindrum, although they were the only two entrants in the latter event because some of the top professionals had established a short-lived rival tournament. He is a member of the New Zealand Sports Hall of Fame.

Name: Clark McConachy, MBE
Born: April 15th 1895
Died: April 12th 1980
Nationality: New Zealander
Turned Pro: 1914 - 1980
Highest Break: 147
Ranking Titles: 0
World Titles: 0

McManus

Alan McManus is one of the most consistent players on the circuit. He enjoyed 16 consecutive years (from when he turned professional in 1990 until 2006) in the world's top 16, although he never quite lived up to his potential. His early form was promising, however, and he ended Stephen Hendry's remarkable five-year unbeaten record at the Masters when he beat his countryman 9-8 in 1994. He also won that year's Dubai Classic, his first ranking trophy.

Above: *Alan McManus at the 2011 Paul Hunter Classic*

McManus could have pushed on and become one of the game's modern greats but, despite reaching 21 professional semi-finals, including two at the Crucible, he only converted them into four victories, one of which was the 1996 Thailand Open. His last major final was the 2002 LG Cup at the Preston Guildhall but he lost 9-5 to Chris Small.

He dropped out of the top 16 after a series of poor results in 2005/06 but he did then reach the semi-final of the Grand Prix. More quiet years followed and he dropped to 52 in the world having failed to qualify for any of the major events in 2011/12. At the 2013 Welsh Open, McManus rolled back the years and reached his first ranking quarter-final since the 2006 Grand Prix after victories over Barry Hawkins and Joe Perry.

Name: Alan McManus
Born: January 21st 1971
Nationality: Scottish
Turned Pro: 1990
Century Breaks: 165
Highest Break: 143
Ranking Titles: 2
World Titles: 0

Meo

Right: *Tony Meo*

Tony Meo and school-friend Jimmy White regularly played truant so they could meet in the local snooker hall. Aged 17, Meo became the youngest person to make a confirmed 147 and, having won the National Under-19 Championship in 1978, he turned professional the following year. He achieved little over the next five years – the only highlight being a win at the non-ranking 1981 Australian Masters – but he then faced Steve Davis in the final of the 1984 Lada Classic. Only needing to clear the colours for victory, Meo was distracted by a drunk spectator and missed an easy pot. Davis won the match and the pair then teamed up to win four world doubles titles.

Meo won his second Australian Masters in 1985 but his only ranking title came at the 1989 British Open when he beat Dean Reynolds in the final. He also reached the semi-final of the World Championship that year but lost 16-7 to John Parrott. His last victory came in the 1990 Matchroom International League but he then slipped down the rankings and retired in 1997.

Name: Tony Meo
Born: October 4th 1959, Tooting
Nationality: English
Turned Pro: 1979 - 1997
Century Breaks: 52
Highest Break: 147
Ranking Titles: 1
World Titles: 0

Miles

Graham Miles had a distinctive style and stance because he was right-handed but left-eyed, so the cue ran to the left of his chin and underneath his left ear. He turned professional in 1969 but had to wait five years before reaching the final of the World Championship. He lost to Ray Reardon 22-12 but then won Pot Black having been given a wildcard entry after Fred Davis withdrew. He won the tournament again in 1975 and then finished runner-up to Reardon at the Masters.

After a couple of quiet years, Miles reached the final of the 1978 UK Championship with notable victories over Rex Williams and Willie Thorne, the latter match seeing him knock in a tournament-best 139 in the final frame. He then lost to Doug Mountjoy in the final, but he made another final appearance at the 1979 Holsten Lager International having seen off John Pulman, Dennis Taylor and Alex Higgins. John Spencer was too strong and took the title, however.

His last major success came at the 1981 Tolly Cobbold Classic but he soon slipped down the rankings and made his final appearance at the Crucible in 1984. He retired in 1992 to run his own snooker clubs but returned for the Senior Pot Black tournament in 1997.

Left: *Graham Miles*

Name: Graham Miles
Born: May 11th 1941, Birmingham
Nationality: English
Turned Pro: 1969 - 1992
Century Breaks: 7
Highest Break: 139
Ranking Titles: 0
World Titles: 0

Morgan

Below: *Darren Morgan*

Darren Morgan won the World Amateur Championship in 1987 and turned professional the following season. He won his first tournament at Pontins in 1989 and then took the 1990 Shootout title. He backed up these minor victories with a semi-final spot at the 1994 World Championships – having beaten Mark King, Willie Thorne and John Parrott – and a hard-fought 9-8 victory over Steve Davis in the final of the 1996 Irish Masters.

Morgan was a solid if unspectacular player and he reached the quarter-finals at the Crucible in 1996 and 1997, but his career then gradually declined until he won the European and World Masters titles in 2007. He then retired from professional snooker, although he entered the 2010 World Open as an amateur and surprised everyone by making the last 64 where he was narrowly beaten 3-2 by Matthew Stevens.

In 2011 he won the World Seniors Title with victories over Cliff Thorburn and Jimmy White. In the final he beat Steve Davis 2-1.

Name: Darren Morgan
Born: May 3rd 1966, Newport
Nationality: Welsh
Turned Pro: 1988 - 2007
Century Breaks: 111
Highest Break: 145
Ranking Titles: 0
World Titles: 0

Mountjoy

Doug Mountjoy started work as a coalminer but he was a precociously talented player who won many amateur events, including the Welsh title and the World Amateur Title in 1976, after which he turned professional at the relatively old age of 34. He made an immediate impact and beat Fred Davis, Alex Higgins and then-world-champion Ray Reardon to win the 1977 Masters.

Mountjoy then beat Higgins again at the World Championship before losing a tight match to Dennis Taylor. At the end of the year he made the final of the inaugural UK Championship, although he narrowly lost to Patsy Fagan. He won the title the following year, however, and also beat Reardon to claim his first Irish Masters title. In 1979 and 1980 he helped Wales win the World Cup, and he continued his good form by beating Ray Reardon in the semi-final at the Crucible in 1981 with a championship-record 145 break.

In the final he faced a young Steve Davis and the Essex man raced into a 6-0 lead, but Mountjoy pegged him back to trail by only two, 11-13. He then missed an easy blue and Davis cleared the remaining colours to pull clear once more. He eventually won 18-12. Mountjoy recovered from the defeat and took the Welsh Professional Title in 1982 and 1984, but he couldn't claim a ranking victory despite reaching the final of the 1985 Masters against Cliff Thorburn.

He won another Welsh title in 1987 but a series of losses put him out of the world's top 16. He employed Coach Frank Callan to help him reach the heights of the early 1980s and he promptly claimed the 1988 UK Championship, his first ranking tournament, with a 16-12 victory over a young Stephen Hendry. He then won the Classic to record back-to-back wins in ranking tournaments, and followed this up with yet another Welsh title.

Having fought his way back, he remained in the top 16 until 1993 and his final World Championship appearance. He beat lung cancer later that year and continued to play on the tour until 1997. He made brief comebacks in 2000 and 2002 but couldn't recapture the form of old.

Name: Doug Mountjoy
Born: June 8th 1942, Glamorgan
Nationality: Welsh
Turned Pro: 1976 - 1997
Century Breaks: 36
Highest Break: 145
Ranking Titles: 2
World Titles: 0

Above: *Doug Mountjoy*

Murphy

Shaun Murphy began playing snooker aged eight when his parents bought him a small table. He made his first century break two years later and then secured a sponsorship deal with the Doc Martens shoe company. He turned professional at 15 and joined the minor UK tour. Several solid performances saw him voted World Snooker Newcomer of the Year in 2000, a year in which he won the English Open.

He won his first professional tournament later the same year at the Benson & Hedges Championship, and he made his first maximum at the same event the following year. He lost to Stephen Hendry, 4-10, in the first round of the 2002 World Championship, and then again the following year to Ken Doherty on the final black, 9-10. He then endured a couple of lean years and was only just ranked in the top 50.

He won a couple of qualifying matches to make it to the Crucible for the 2005 World Championship but he was a complete outsider – some bookies were offering 150-1 – and wasn't given any chance in the tournament proper. He promptly dispatched a list of former champions, including John Higgins, Steve Davis and Peter Ebdon, to reach the final against Matthew Stevens. He trailed 6-10 at the end of the first day but turned the tables on the Welshman to draw level at 16-16 late in the final session. He then knocked in two frame-winning breaks to lift the trophy. He was another victim of the Crucible Curse when he was knocked out in the quarter-final of his defence by Peter Ebdon, however.

He was now firmly established in the top 16 and he won the 2007 Malta Cup, but he couldn't squeeze past Mark Selby in the semi-final of the World Championship. His run in the tournament took him up to world number three and he justified his position by reaching five ranking semi-finals in 2007/08, although he didn't win another event until successfully defending the Malta Cup.

He was one of the favourites for the 2008 World Championship but was beaten in the second round by Ali Carter. Several poor performances were attributed to personal problems but he eventually rediscovered his form and won the 2008 UK Championship, only the tenth player to have done the UK and World double. He then reached the final of the 2009 World Championship after victories over Andrew Higginson, Marco Fu, Stephen Hendry and Neil Robertson, but he was soundly beaten 18-9 by John Higgins for the title.

The following season he defended the Paul Hunter Classic and won the Premier League, but his form then inexplicably dipped and he went out in the first round of a number of ranking events and dropped to world number seven. He stormed back with victories at the Wuxi Classic and Brugge Open, as well as reaching the final of the Ruhr Championship and the Premier League, and the semi-final of the World Championship.

He reached the latter stages of several ranking events but couldn't win another title until he whitewashed Graeme Dott 5-0 in the final of the 2011 Brazil Masters. He then reached his first Masters final but lost 6-10 to an in-form Neil Robertson. He ended the season poorly and began 2012/13 in the same vein, but he soon upped his game and reached the semi-final at the Shanghai Masters and the International Championship. He also made the final of the UK Championship – although he lost to Mark Selby, 6-10 – and the semi-final of the Masters. He then made the quarter-final of the World Championship but was narrowly beaten by Judd Trump.

Murphy has a bitter rivalry with Stephen Maguire, which stems from their meeting in the 2004 Grand Prix. Maguire forgot his chalk so the match had to be delayed by a few minutes. Murphy spoke to the referee and the tournament director docked Maguire a frame for not being ready to start on time. Maguire won the match and then said he didn't want to be a fat world champion. Murphy has also criticised Ding Junhui, amongst others, for having too many toilet breaks, and Ronnie O'Sullivan for being unprofessional and undeserving of his popularity.

A devout Christian, Murphy has donated more than £100,000 to the church.

Left: *Shaun Murphy at the 2012 Masters*

Name: Shaun Murphy
Born: August 10th 1982, Harlow
Nationality: English
Turned Pro: 1998
Century Breaks: 263
Highest Break: 147
Ranking Titles: 4
World Titles: 1

O'Brien

Below: *Fergal O'Brien takes on a difficult blue*

Far Right: *New Zealander Dene O'Kane*

Fergal O'Brien is another journeyman professional, always solid but rarely spectacular. It took him eight years as a pro before he finally won a ranking event, the 1999 British Open, against Anthony Hamilton (he won five frames on the final black to clinch the title). He also made the final of the 2001 Masters, although he ran into an inspired Paul Hunter, with the Leeds man battling back from 3-7 to take the title.

O'Brien flirted with the top 16 for a couple of seasons, and became the only player to knock in a century in his first frame at the Crucible (against Alan McManus in 1994). Despite this, he only ever made the quarter-final of the World Championship. He qualified for the Shanghai Masters and the Grand Prix in 2007 but couldn't progress to the latter stages of the tournaments. He then reached the final of the ranking Northern Ireland Trophy but he lost to Stephen Maguire, 5-9. This run saw him re-enter the top 32 but his recent form has been patchy at best and he could only manage wins in two minor tournaments, the 2010 Irish Classic and the 2011 Lucan Racing Classic.

Name: Fergal O'Brien
Born: March 8th 1972
Nationality: Irish
Turned Pro: 1991
Century Breaks: 145
Highest Break: 143
Ranking Titles: 1
World Titles: 0

O'Kane

Dene O'Kane turned professional in 1984 after a solid amateur career in New Zealand. Three years later he surprised the establishment by qualifying for the World Championship at his first attempt, although he lost to David Taylor in the first round. In 1987 he reached the quarter-final at the Crucible and also entered the world's top 32 players. He was runner-up to Mike Hallett at the 1989 Hong Kong Open, then qualified again for the World Championship in 1992, after which he gradually slipped down the rankings.

Name: Dene O'Kane
Born: February 24th 1963
Nationality: New Zealander
Turned Pro: 1984
Century Breaks: 46
Highest Break: 140
Ranking Titles: 0
World Titles: 0

O'Sullivan

Ronnie O'Sullivan was born in the Midlands but then moved to Chigwell in Essex. His snooker career started when he knocked in a century aged only 10, and he won his first pro-am tournament two years later. His first maximum came at 15 so he turned professional the following year. He promptly won his first 38 ranking matches en route to the 1993 World Championship, a record that still stands. He was knocked out in the first round by Alan McManus but he collected his first ranking tournament with victory at the UK Championship later that year. In 1995 he won his first Masters.

O'Sullivan's career reached new heights when he knocked in a maximum break in the first round of the 1997 World Championship in only five minutes twenty seconds. Later that year he won his second UK title. He also made it to the semi-final of the 1999 World Championship but he lost 13-17 to Stephen Hendry. Repeated failures at the biggest event could have inhibited normal players but O'Sullivan was too good not to win the world crown.

In the 2000/01 season he claimed six titles, including the elusive World Championship after beating John Higgins 18-14 in a tense final. He also succumbed to the famous Crucible Curse when Stephen Hendry knocked him out in the semi-final of his defence, but a strong overall season saw him ranked number one in the world. On his day, he was untouchable and once knocked in five centuries in a best of nine frame match.

In 2002/03 he started quietly but then won back-to-back ranking titles at the European Open and Irish Masters. After a slight dip in form, Ray Reardon was drafted in to help guide O'Sullivan and he promptly won his second world title after an 18-8 demolition of Graeme Dott in the final. He then won his second Masters title against John Higgins (10-3), after which the Scotsman described him as a 'total genius'.

Several erratic seasons followed but he won his share of tournaments, including a record seventh Premier League title in 2007 and another UK Championship later in a year in which he also knocked in his eighth competitive maximum. He won his third world title the following May with an 18-8 mauling of Ali Carter, although Carter had some revenge by halving

Left: *Ronnie O'Sullivan takes on a tough plant at the 2012 German Masters*

O'Sullivan's prize money for the high break as they both knocked in maximums. He then won his fourth Masters to equal Stephen Hendry's record.

During an exhibition match in early 2009, he and Jimmy White made consecutive maximums. He made another 147 at the 2010 World Open, although referee Jan Verhaas had to persuade him to knock in the final black because O'Sullivan knew there was no bonus money for a maximum.

He again endured several highs and lows before entering the 2012 World Championship. In his first three matches he beat former champions Peter Ebdon, Mark Williams and Neil Robertson, and then saw off Matthew Stevens and Ali Carter to claim the title for a fourth time. At 36, he was the oldest champion since Ray Reardon (45) in 1978. He then refused to sign the players' contract and withdrew from almost every event in the season, although he did finally sign up and promised to defend his world title in 2013.

He was in imperious form at the Crucible and comfortably beat Marcus Campbell, Ali Carter, Stuart Bingham, Judd Trump and then Barry Hawkins in the final to claim his fifth world title. In all he knocked in 13 centuries, with a record six in the final itself, and looked to have benefited from his year away from the game.

O'Sullivan is probably the most naturally gifted player to pick up a cue. He

Above: *O'Sullivan 2013*

plays aggressively and compiles monster breaks with ease. His safety play is also now among the best but he regularly plays left handed to avoid using the rest – he has notched several century breaks with his 'wrong' hand.

O'Sullivan's career has been blighted by problems, however: In 1996 he was found guilty of assaulting media official Mike Ganley; he then consistently played left handed in a match against Alain Robidoux, which the Canadian found disrespectful, but O'Sullivan claimed he was better than Robidoux with either hand; he was stripped of the 1998 Irish Masters title having tested positive for cannabis; he vowed to retire after complaining about Peter Ebdon's painfully slow play in their 2005 World Championship quarter-final; in December 2006 he conceded his best-of-17 quarter-final at the UK Championship to Stephen Hendry despite being only 4-1 down because he'd 'had enough'; he refused to speak to the media after beating Ali Carter at the 2007 Masters; at a press conference after his first-round elimination at the 2008 China Open he made lewd comments and was fined by the WPBSA; and he then described the organisation as a 'cancer running through the game'.

If he can keep a clear head and concentrate on the game, there's no doubt that O'Sullivan can still challenge for the World Championship for some years to come.

Name: Ronnie O'Sullivan
Born: December 5th 1975, West Midlands
Nationality: English
Turned Pro: 1992
Century Breaks: 691
Highest Break: 147
Ranking Titles: 25
World Titles: 5

Owen

Gary Owen first came to prominence when he won the British Under-16 Champion in 1944. In 1950 he reached the final of the English Amateur Championship but he then retired from competition until 1963 when he finally took the title. Having qualified for the World Amateur Championships in Calcutta, he won all his matches. He won the title for a second time three years later by beating John Spencer in the final.

In 1968 he turned professional along with Spencer and Ray Reardon, but he lost to Spencer in the following year's World Championship final. He reached the semi-final again in 1970 and the last eight in 1972 and 1975, although by then he was living in Australia, a country he eventually represented at the World Cup in 1979.

Above: *John Spencer watches Gary Owen break off in the final of the 1969 World Championship*

Name: Gary Owen
Born: 1929, Carmarthenshire
Died: 1995, Brisbane
Nationality: Welsh
Turned Pro: 1968 - 1995
Highest Break: 147
Ranking Titles: 0
World Titles: 0

Parrott

Below: *John Parrott*

John Parrott began his sporting career playing bowls but he discovered snooker aged 12 and attracted manager Phil Miller three years later. He made the final of the English Under-16 amateur tournament in 1980 and was Junior Pot Black champion in 1982 and 1983. Having won 14 titles in his last year as an amateur, he turned professional and made his television debut at the 1984 Classic against Alex Higgins in Warrington.

He beat Higgins and Tony Knowles before losing to Steve Davis in the semi-final, but he soon had his first ranking title in the bag when he won the 1989 European Open. He then made the final of the World Championship but he was demolished 18-3 by Steve Davis, the biggest winning margin in modern times. Having defended the European Open title the following year he was ready for another crack at the world title. This time he delivered and overcame Jimmy White in the final to be crowned 1991 World Champion. Later that year he added the UK Championship, one of only five players to win both in the same calendar year. He also won the Dubai Classic.

Had it not been for Stephen Hendry's dominance he might also have won the Masters but he only managed to finish runner-up three times to the Scotsman. He defended the Dubai Classic in 1992 and added the International Open in 1994. His last two ranking victories came at the 1995 Thailand Classic and the 1996 European Open.

He reached the last 16 at the Crucible every year until 1995, but then his career began a slow decline. He came through the World Championship qualifying event a record ten times, and the same number of his matches at the Crucible have been decided on the final frame, also a record. He was beaten in the qualifiers for the 2010 World Championship and dropped out of the top 64, however. As he was no longer assured a place on the main tour, he decided to retire.

Parrott has been a television personality for much of his career and he was a team captain on the BBC's A Question of Sport from 1996 until 2002. He is also a horse-racing fan and part-time pundit.

Name: John Parrott, MBE
Born: May 11th 1964, Liverpool
Nationality: English
Turned Pro: 1983 - 2010
Century Breaks: 221
Highest Break: 147
Ranking Titles: 9
World Titles: 1

Perry

Joe Perry made a steady start to his professional career and he reached the last 16 on his World Championship debut in 1999 with a victory over Steve Davis. He eventually reached his first final at the 2001 European Open although he was comprehensively beaten 9-2 by Stephen Hendry. The following season he cracked the top 16 and enjoyed a run to the quarter-final of the 2004 World Championship after beating defending champion Mark Williams, 13-11. He also won the prize for the highest break with a 145.

He then had a couple of quiet seasons – his best performances were semi-final berths at the 2004 and 2005 UK Championships – before making another run at the Crucible in 2008 when he beat Graeme Dott, Stuart Bingham and Stephen Maguire on his way to the semi-final. He was beaten by Ali Carter but his recent results saw him return to the elite top 16.

He confirmed his status by beating Ronnie O'Sullivan at the UK Championship later that year but he then lost to Marco Fu in the quarter-final. He reached the same stage at the Players' Tour Championship in 2011/12 but a string of poor results saw him slide down the rankings to number 24. He still managed to win the World Mixed Doubles title with Tatjana Vasiljeva in 2010 and 2011, however.

Left: *Joe Perry*

Name: Joe Perry
Born: August 13th 1974, Wisbech
Nationality: English
Turned Pro: 1991
Century Breaks: 150
Highest Break: 145
Ranking Titles: 0
World Titles: 0

Pinches

Right: *Barry Pinches at the 2007 Paul Hunter Classic*

Barry Pinches won the English Amateur Championship in 1988 and immediately turned professional. Although he qualified for the 1991 World Championship, he was soundly beaten 3-10 by Terry Griffiths and didn't make much of an impact in his first decade as a pro. It was only when he beat Jimmy White 10-8 and ran Stephen Hendry close (12-13) at the same event 13 years later that he became a household name. This gap between Crucible appearances remains a record.

In 2003 he had enjoyed a run to the quarter-final of the UK Championship after beating Marco Fu, Graeme Dott and Stephen Lee, but Stephen Hendry ended his hopes of a first ranking title. He did break into the top 16 but slipped down the rankings and out of the top 32 having changed his cue action.

He came back with a win at the 2007 Paul Hunter Classic and reached the last 16 of the 2008 China Open. He then narrowly missed out on what would have been his second maximum – his first came at the 2000 Welsh Open – when he faltered on the final black. A run of poor performances saw him fall to number 64 by the beginning of the 2012/13 season.

Name: Barry Pinches
Born: July 13th 1970, Norwich
Nationality: English
Turned Pro: 1989
Century Breaks: 118
Highest Break: 147
Ranking Titles: 0
World Titles: 0

Pulman

John Pulman was a prodigious talent who won the 1946 English Amateur Title before turning professional. He was soundly beaten in his first assault on the world title and didn't win a tournament until the 1951 Empire News Event. Four years later he reached the final of the World Matchplay but he wasn't quite good enough to trouble Fred Davis either then or the following year.

In 1964 the World Championship restarted as a challenge event. Pulman won the inaugural title and defended it six times over the next four years. In 1969 it reverted to a knockout tournament and Pulman reached the final in 1970, although he lost to Ray Reardon. He enjoyed another run at the Crucible in 1977 at the age of 54, but he lost in the semi-final to eventual winner John Spencer, 16-18.

Two years later, after a series of poor results, he was declared bankrupt. He retired in 1982 and was a leading television commentator for the next decade. He died after a fall at home in 1998 but he will long be remembered as one of the finest players to grace the green baize.

Name: John Pulman
Born: December 12th 1923
Died: December 25th 1998
Nationality: English
Turned Pro: 1946 - 1982
Ranking Titles: 10
World Titles: 7

Above: *One of the all-time greats, John Pulman, gives Alex Higgins some advice*

Rea

Right: *Jackie Rea*

Jackie Rea started playing at the age of nine in the billiard room of his father's pub. He was naturally gifted and soon won the All-Ireland, Northern Irish, and Irish Professional titles, holding the latter until being beaten by Alex Higgins 20 years later in 1972. He tried to stop snooker slipping into decline in the 1950s and ended up losing narrowly in the World Championship on several occasions to John Pulman.

He won the 1955 News of the World Championship by winning all eight matches, a feat only previously achieved by Joe Davis. With interest in the sport still on the wane, Rea played hundreds of exhibition matches, delivering one-liners while executing a variety of trick shots. Indeed John Virgo and Dennis Taylor both cite Rea as the inspiration for some of their comedy routines.

He entered the modern era's first World Championship in 1969 but lost to Gary Owen. He ran John Spencer close the following year and was a regular fixture at the event until the 1980s, although by then his powers had diminished. He still managed to beat future World Champion Joe Johnson in the 1982 Golden Leisure Classic and also made it to the quarter-final of the 1985 Irish Professional Championship.

Having been knocked out of the qualifying tournament for the 1991 World Championship, Rea hung up his cue and devoted his time to coaching.

Name: Jackie Rea
Born: April 6th 1921, County Tyrone
Nationality: Northern Irish
Turned Pro: 1947 - 1991
Highest Break: 146
Ranking Titles: 0
World Titles: 0

Reardon

Ray Reardon was born into a mining community, and he was working in the pits aged 14 because he wanted to play snooker in his spare time rather than go to grammar school. He quit the job after being buried by a rock fall and would later become a policeman in Stoke-on-Trent. Reardon was a talented snooker player and he won the British Youth Championship at 15, and then the Welsh Amateur Title for six years (1950-55).

He finally beat John Spencer to the English Amateur Title in 1964 and went on an exhibition tour to South Africa. The trip was so successful that he turned professional. He won the first Pot Black tournament in 1969 and then his first world crown in 1970. He was now a household name, and he was developing into the finest player of his generation. He won six world titles, including four in succession in the 1970s, bringing a mix of humour, great skill and tactical nous to the table.

He enjoyed a number of titanic tussles with John Spencer – particularly their semi-final in 1973, which Reardon won 23-22 – and Eddie Charlton, who Reardon beat 31-30 in the epic 1975 world final. His incredible run was finally halted in the first Crucible World Championship in 1977 when he was beaten by John Spencer in the quarter-final, the first time he had lost since being beaten by Rex Williams in 1972. He regained the title the following year, however, by beating Doug Mountjoy, Bill Werbeniuk, Eddie Charlton and then Perrie Mans in the final.

He won the one-off Champion of Champions event in 1978, then regained his Pot Black title the following year, and he finally won the World Challenge Cup for Wales alongside Mountjoy and Terry Griffiths. But the writing was on the wall for the old guard. Newcomers like Steve Davis and Jimmy White were preparing to dominate in the 1980s.

Reardon enjoyed an Indian Summer to his career, however: he whitewashed Davis twice, returned to number one in the rankings, reached the 1982 world final, won the Players' Professional Tournament, reached the final of the Benson & Hedges

Masters, and then regained the Welsh Title with a 9-1 hammering of Mountjoy. His last run at the Crucible came in 1985 when he reached the semi-final. He finally retired when his sight began to falter in the early 1990s, although he did play a senior event in 2000.

The likeable Welshman, known as Dracula for his toothy smile and widow's peak, ushered the game into the modern era. He was a supreme long potter, break-builder and tactician whose influence on the game cannot be underestimated. He maintains an active interest today, and helped mentor Ronnie O'Sullivan when the latter was struggling psychologically and technically.

Name: Ray Reardon, MBE
Born: October 8th 1932, Tredegar
Nationality: Welsh
Turned Pro: 1967 - 1992
Century Breaks: 27
Highest Break: 146
Ranking Titles: 5
World Titles: 6

Reynolds

Dean Reynolds won the first Junior Pot Black by beating Dene O'Kane in 1981. He immediately turned professional but couldn't make much of an impact on the tour. He reached two ranking finals in 1989, however, but lost them both, the first to Tony Meo at the British Open and the second to Steve Davis at the Grand Prix. Reynolds is one of very few players to have made a 16-red total clearance after his opponent fouled and left him a free ball (he knocked in a 143 at the 2006 European Team Championship). He suffered a stroke in 2009 but continued to play having relearned the sport.

Name: Dean Reynolds
Born: January 11th 1963, Grimsby
Nationality: English
Turned Pro: 1981
Century Breaks: 40
Highest Break: 143
Ranking Titles: 0
World Titles: 0

Left: *Dean Reynolds*

Far Left: *Ray Reardon was a six-time World Champion in the 1970s*

Robertson

Below: *Neil Robertson celebrates winning the 2012 Masters*

Neil Robertson made his first century break at the age of 14. Three years later he reached the third qualifying round for the 1999 World Championship but he couldn't reach the tournament proper and endured a couple of quiet seasons. In 2003 he won the Under-21 World Championship and earned a place on the main tour. By the end of the following season he was ranked in the top 32 and reached the final stages of six out of the eight main events.

By 2005/06 he was a major force and he entered the world's top 16 by reaching four quarter-finals, including the World Championship. He won his first ranking event, the 2006 Grand Prix, after victories over Ronnie O'Sullivan, Alan McManus and Jamie Cope. He backed this up with victory at the Welsh Open but then had a couple of poor seasons.

He bounced back at the 2009 World Championship with wins over Steve Davis, Ali Carter and Stephen Maguire, but Shaun Murphy proved too strong in the semi-final (14-17). Robertson put the disappointment behind him and won the

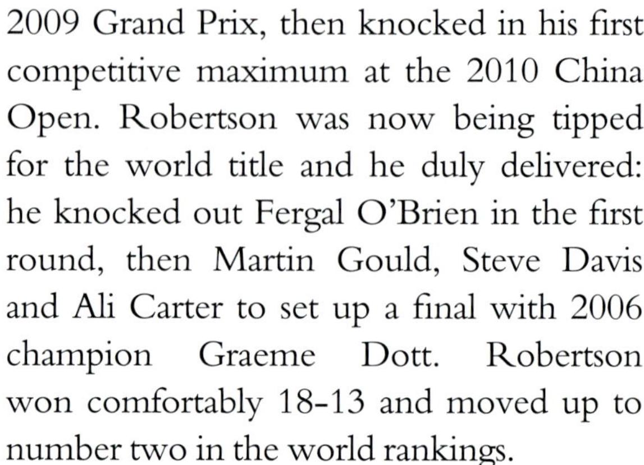

2009 Grand Prix, then knocked in his first competitive maximum at the 2010 China Open. Robertson was now being tipped for the world title and he duly delivered: he knocked out Fergal O'Brien in the first round, then Martin Gould, Steve Davis and Ali Carter to set up a final with 2006 champion Graeme Dott. Robertson won comfortably 18-13 and moved up to number two in the world rankings.

He promptly won the World Open but couldn't defend his world title and was knocked out in the first round by Judd Trump: the famous curse had struck again. He recovered from the defeat and won two PTC events and the Masters in 2011/12, and then the China Open the following season, a win which saw him move back to world number two.

Despite losing again in the first round of the 2013 World Championship, the brilliant Australian is now at the peak of his ability and will surely claim more ranking titles.

Name: Neil Robertson
Born: February 11th 1982, Melbourne
Nationality: Australian
Turned Pro: 1998
Century Breaks: 256
Highest Break: 147
Ranking Titles: 7
World Titles: 1

Robidoux

Above: *Trick-shot specialist Alain Robidoux*

Alain Robidoux started off as a non-tournament professional, which meant he was listed on the world rankings but couldn't enter most of the events. By 1988 he'd amassed enough ranking points to join the tour full-time and he immediately knocked in a 147 during that year's European Open. His best performance in a ranking event came at the 1996 German Open, although he was beaten by Ronnie O'Sullivan in the final.

He and O'Sullivan almost came to blows in the first round of that year's World Championship when the Englishman repeatedly played left-handed. Robidoux thought he was being disrespectful and refused to shake his hand at the end of the match, which the Canadian had lost 3-10. Robidoux made a formal complaint but O'Sullivan responded by claiming he could play better than the Canadian with either hand. The WPBSA intervened and asked O'Sullivan to play former World Billiards Champion Rex Williams in a best-of-five-frame match so they could assess how good he was with his left hand. O'Sullivan won 3-0 and the disciplinary charges were dropped.

Robidoux reached the semi-final of the 1997 World Championship and looked set to become a major force in the game, but he then sent his cue back to its maker for a few minor repairs. When the elderly manufacturer noticed that the butt now had a 'Riley' logo stamped on it, he smashed the cue and posted it back to Robidoux in pieces. The Canadian's game fell apart and he plummeted down the rankings.

Robidoux is a trick-shot specialist who is known for his impressions of leading players like Steve Davis, Dennis Taylor and Alex Higgins.

Name: Alain Robidoux
Born: July 25th 1960, Quebec
Nationality: Canadian
Turned Pro: 1988
Century Breaks: 37
Highest Break: 147
Ranking Titles: 0
World Titles: 0

Roe

Below: *David Roe*

David Roe's professional career began promisingly and in only his second year he was ranked in the world's top 32. In 1988 he reached the last 16 of the World Championship on his Crucible debut, and he also scooped the BBC's 'Shot of the Championship' for an exquisite long pot.

Roe then made it to two quarter-finals in 1991/92 and squeezed into the elite top 16, where he would remain for three years. After several first-round defeats, he slid out of the top 32 and made little impact on the tour for the next decade. In 2005, however, he reached the last 16 of the China Open, but this proved to be a flash in the pan and he dropped off the tour in 2010 to concentrate on coaching the Iranian national team.

Name: David Roe
Born: September 11th 1965
Nationality: English
Turned Pro: 1986 - 2010
Century Breaks: 42
Highest Break: 140
Ranking Titles: 0
World Titles: 0

Selby

Mark Selby was an inconsistent player as a teenager but he joined the second-tier UK tour in 1998. It took him four years to reach the semi-final of a ranking event, the 2002 China Open, but he then made the final of the Regal Scottish event in 2003 before losing to David Gray 9-7. He was unable to qualify for the World Championships until 2005, but, having made it to the Crucible, he went out in the first round to John Higgins.

Selby avenged this defeat the following year by beating Higgins 10-4 but he then lost to Mark Williams. He and Higgins were destined to meet at the Crucible again the following year, with much more riding on their third meeting: Selby dispatched Stephen Lee, Peter Ebdon, Ali Carter and Shaun Murphy to set up a final against the Scotsman. Higgins raced out of the blocks and was soon 12-4 ahead but Selby rallied and won six frames on the spin. He closed to within one frame at 13-14 but Higgins then eased clear to win 18-13.

Selby's solid showing saw him move into the top 16, and he backed this up with a semi-final slot at the UK Championship, although he was narrowly beaten by Ronnie O'Sullivan who knocked in a 147 in the deciding frame. In early 2008 Selby beat Stephen Hendry, Stephen Maguire, Ken Doherty and Stephen Lee to win his first major title, the Masters, at Wembley. He then won his second at the Welsh Open, and his second Masters in 2010.

Selby's incredible form continued when he made the final of the 2011 China Open (he lost 10-8 to Judd Trump), and he then knocked in a record six centuries in his second-round match against Stephen Hendry at the World Championship. His total of 55 for the season was another record. He then won the Wuxi Classic, the Shanghai Masters and the Paul Hunter Classic to claim the world number one spot.

However, a neck injury hampered his progress and he withdrew from the China Open and lost in the first round of the World Championship. He lost the top spot to Judd Trump but regained it

by winning the 2012 UK Championship, then defending the Paul Hunter Classic and also claiming the Munich Open and his third Masters.

At the 2013 China Open, Selby became only the fourth person to miss the final black in a 147 attempt, although he still went on to reach the final. He is still ranked number one in the world and, now that his neck injury has cleared up, will surely challenge for the major honours in 2013/14. He was a surprise casualty in the second round of the World Championship, however.

Selby is also a keen darts player – he beat Eric Bristow in an exhibition in 2007 – and he won the World 8-ball Pool Championship in 2006.

Name: Mark Selby
Born: June 19th 1983, Leicester
Nationality: English
Turned Pro: 1998
Century Breaks: 290
Highest Break: 147
Ranking Titles: 3
World Titles: 0

Small

Chris Small may have been the youngest player to win on his Crucible debut – he beat Doug Mountjoy aged 18 in 1992 – but he had a relatively low profile on the professional tour until the 2002 LG Cup. He defied the odds to beat Ronnie O'Sullivan and John Higgins before edging out Alan McManus in the final. However, he was then diagnosed with the debilitating spinal condition ankylosing spondylitis, a chronic inflammatory disease where the vertebrae fuse together.

He managed to enter the top 16 but had to pull out of his World Championship match with Alan McManus in 2005 because the steroid injections in his neck were affecting his vision. His condition deteriorated and he was forced to retire at the end of the season. He applied to the WPBSA for a grant from the organisation's trust fund to help him cope but his application was refused. Despite being heavily criticised for its decision by several top players, the governing body has refused to reverse its ruling.

Name: Chris Small
Born: September 26th 1973
Nationality: Scottish
Turned Pro: 1991 - 2005
Century Breaks: 54
Highest Break: 141
Ranking Titles: 1
World Titles: 0

Above: *Chris Small with the 2002 LG Cup*

Far Left: *Mark Selby wins the 2012 Paul Hunter Classic*

Smith, Sidney

Right: *A commemorative Sidney Smith cue*

Sidney Smith was one of the greatest pre-war players. He knocked in a world record 133 break in 1936 at the Thurston Snooker Handicap Tournament, and he was the first man to make a total clearance with a break of 136 at the Daily Mail Gold Cup in 1939 (he reached the final of this tournament twice). He came second to Joe Davis in the 1938 world final having beaten Joe's brother Fred 18-13 in the semi-final. He was runner up to Joe again the following year, and he made another semi-final in 1940.

He continued in the same vein after the war, reaching the semi-finals again in 1947 and 1949. Joe Davis continually thwarted him, however, and he was second again to the great man at the prestigious 1950 News of the World Championship. He was also a prolific billiards player and recorded three 1,000+ breaks, his best being 1,292.

Name: Sidney Smith
Born: March 26th 1908, Derbyshire
Died: 1990
Nationality: English
Turned Pro: 1930
Highest Break: 136
Ranking Titles: 0
World Titles: 0

Smith, Willie

Willie Smith will forever be remembered as the greatest billiards player of all time. He first entered the World Championship in 1920, winning easily, but arguments with the governing body prevented him from entering again until 1923. He won that year's tournament and promptly turned to snooker to avoid any further conflict with the authorities and to earn a little money from the sport. Although he was not in the same class as a snooker player, he was still good enough to reach the World Snooker Final in 1933 and 1935. He was beaten on both occasions by the greatest player of his generation, Joe Davis.

Smith continued to play both sports and by the end of the 1920s his billiard records were unapproachable: a high break of 2,743, fifteen breaks over 1,000 in one season, and 83 four-figure breaks by 1932 (in a match against Sidney Smith in Manchester he made seven 1,000+ breaks in a week).

Name: Willie Smith
Born: January 25th 1886, Darlington
Died: June 2nd 1982, Leeds
Nationality: English
Turned Pro: 1920
Ranking Titles: 0
World Titles: 0

Above: *A Willie Smith & George Nelson billiard table*

Spencer

John Spencer's promising early career was hindered by the decline in interest in the sport and, having started playing at 15, he couldn't turn professional until the game began its revival when he was 33. He was runner-up to Ray Reardon in his first ever tournament, the 1964 English Amateur Championship, but eventually lifted the trophy two years later.

Spencer then borrowed £100 from his bank to enter the 1969 World Championship. He beat defending champion John Pulman in the first round and then saw off Rex Williams and Gary Owen to claim the title at his first attempt. Only Joe Davis (at the inaugural World Championship in 1927) had previously achieved this, although Alex Higgins (1972) and Terry Griffiths (1979) would equal the feat.

Ray Reardon took his title the following year but Spencer won it back in 1971 by making three centuries in four frames against Warren Simpson in the final. He also won the Pot Black tournament three times. Snooker finally became the popular spectator sport it is today when Spencer and Alex Higgins contested an epic final of the 1972 World Championship. The week-long event was eventually clinched by Higgins (37-32) with hundreds of people crammed into the British Legion in Selly Oak, Birmingham.

Spencer won the inaugural Masters in 1975 and, when the World Championship moved to the Crucible in 1977, he won the title for the third time having seen off John Virgo, Ray Reardon, John Pulman and then Cliff Thorburn. Although his fortunes at the Crucible declined, Spencer was still capable of winning tournaments: the first Irish Masters, the Warners Open, the Castle Professional and the 1979 Holsten Lager International. In the latter event he knocked in the first ever maximum in tournament play, although it wasn't televised because the film crew had been given the afternoon off.

He won his last solo event at the Australian Masters in 1980, although

Below: *Three-time World Champion John Spencer*

he then helped Steve Davis and David Taylor to the World Team Classic. He enjoyed the odd minor success but his career then gradually declined, due in part to problems with his sight. He made his last Crucible appearance in 1986 but lost to old rival Alex Higgins, 10-7.

He was a welcome addition to the commentary box in 1978 but poor health saw him retire in 1998. He was then diagnosed with stomach cancer, although he refused treatment so he could live without the debilitating effects of chemotherapy. He died a year after appearing at the 2005 Champions' Parade at the Crucible.

Name: John Spencer
Born: September 18th 1935, Radcliffe
Died: July 11th 2006, Radcliffe
Nationality: English
Turned Pro: 1968 - 1992
Century Breaks: 25
Highest Break: 147
Ranking Titles: 1
World Titles: 3

Stevens, Kirk

Below: *Kirk Stevens*

Kirk Stevens knocked in his first century at the tender age of 12, although it took him another eight years to turn professional. Then, still aged only 21, he reached the semi-final of the 1980 World Championship, although he was beaten by Alex Higgins, 13-16. Four years later he made the first televised maximum in the Benson & Hedges Masters, the only 147 in the tournament until Ding Junhui equalled it in 2007.

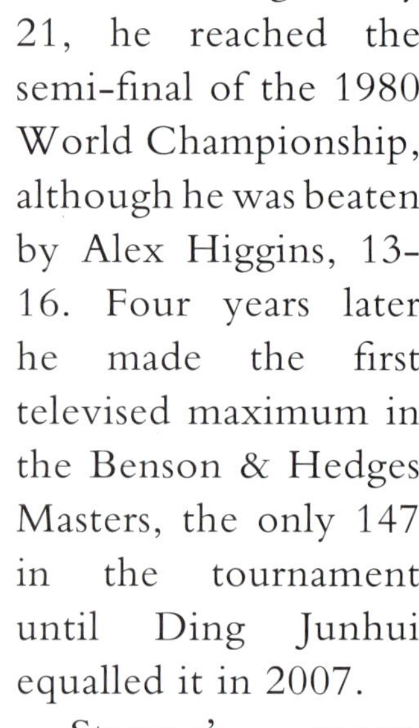

Stevens's career looked to be on the up when he was accused by Silvino Francisco of taking stimulants in the final of the British Open, which Francisco won 12-9. The South African was fined by the WPBSA for his comments but, despite not failing a dope test, Stevens admitted to a cocaine addiction shortly afterwards. He underwent treatment but his career was in freefall and he subsequently dropped out of the world's top 16.

He played on for another five years but then returned to Canada and retired. He made a brief comeback in 1998/99 but dropped off the tour the following season. He still plays regularly and won the Canadian National Championship in 1997, 1998, 2000, 2002 and 2008. He returned to the Crucible for a Legends tournament before the 2011 World Championship.

Name: Kirk Stevens
Born: August 17th 1958
Nationality: Canadian
Turned Pro: 1978
Century Breaks: 24
Highest Break: 147
Ranking Titles: 0
World Titles: 0

Stevens, Matthew

Matthew Stevens made an immediate impact on the professional circuit. He won the Benson & Hedges Championship and qualified for the 1996 Masters, winning his first match against Terry Griffiths but then losing to Alan McManus. He continued his good start by beating Stephen Hendry 5-1 in the Grand Prix and reaching the semi-final of the following year's UK Championship. He also reached the quarter-final in his first World Championship after victories over Alain Robidoux and Mark King. His first ranking final was the 1998 UK Championship, although he lost 6-10 to John Higgins.

In 2000 he won the Masters and, having beaten Tony Drago, Alan McManus, Jimmy White and Joe Swail, he reached his first World Championship final. He led compatriot Mark Williams 10-6 and 14-10, but then caved in and was eventually beaten 18-16. He recovered from the defeat to reach the semi-finals again in 2001 and 2002. In the latter match against Peter Ebdon he only needed a simple red to leave Ebdon needing snookers but he missed the pot and the Englishman cleared up. Ebdon then took the next two frames and won the match.

Stevens bounced back again and won his only ranking title to date, the 2003 UK Championship against Stephen Hendry. A poor season was punctuated by another solid showing at the 2004 World Championship where he again made the semi-final. The agony continued the following year when he reached the final against an un-fancied Shaun Murphy.

He had Murphy on the rack and was four frames up, but Murphy then rallied to 11-12. Stevens then played the final blue in frame 22 left handed rather than use the rest, and missed. Murphy seized the opportunity and cleared up. With the momentum now in his favour, he denied Stevens the title with an 18-16 win. Murphy was his nemesis again in 2007. Stevens was 12-7 ahead in the best of 25 quarter-final but he lost six frames on the bounce and dropped out of the top 16 for the first time in nearly a decade.

Right: *Welshman Matthew Stevens has twice finished runner-up at the World Championships*

After a couple of quiet seasons, Stevens seemed to be getting back to his best and he enjoyed runs to the quarter-finals of 2010/11 Shanghai Masters and Welsh Open before winning the Championship League. Despite staying out of the top 16 after a number of poor results, Stevens beat Marco Fu, Barry Hawkins and Ryan Day to reach his sixth semi-final at the World Championships in 2012. In his quarter-final he rattled off 11 consecutive frames to set up a meeting with Ronnie O'Sullivan.

Although he went down 10-17 to O'Sullivan, he was provisionally ranked 10 in the world, his highest placing since 2005. In the lead-up to the 2013 World Championships his ranking slipped to 12 but he was still exempt from qualifying. He is also a keen poker player and won the UK's richest Texas Hold 'em tournament in 2004.

Name: Matthew Stevens
Born: September 11th 1977, Carmarthen
Nationality: Welsh
Turned Pro: 1994
Century Breaks: 241
Highest Break: 147
Ranking Titles: 1
World Titles: 0

Swail

Joe Swail was English Amateur Champion in 1990 and Northern Irish Amateur runner up so he turned professional in 1991. He entered the world's top 16 after only three years but immediately dropped down the rankings after registering only two wins in the entire 1997/98 season. He bounced back in considerable style by reaching the semi-final of the 2000 and 2001 World Championships but he was beaten by Matthew Stevens and Ronnie O'Sullivan respectively.

His rollercoaster continued after another three poor seasons and he only briefly flirted with the top 16 after victory at the Irish Championships in 2005. He then beat Judd Trump in the qualifying campaign for the 2008 World Championship and thrashed Stephen Lee in the opening match at the tournament proper. He was 8-12 down to Liang Wenbo in the second round but fought back to 12-12 and would have won the match had he knocked in an easy brown.

He had to wait until the following season to reach his first ranking final, the 2009 Welsh Open. He was 5-2 up against Ali Carter but then lost seven consecutive frames and the match.

Swail's hearing is impaired but he considers this an advantage at tournaments like the World Championship because he doesn't get distracted by the crowd and other background noise. Indeed this may be the reason his record at the Crucible was so good. He retired in 2012 although he regularly plays exhibitions with his distinctive and unorthodox style.

Above: *The 'Outlaw' Joe Swail*

Name: Joe Swail
Born: August 29th 1969, Belfast
Nationality: Northern Irish
Turned Pro: 1991 - 2012
Century Breaks: 98
Highest Break: 142
Ranking Titles: 0
World Titles: 0

Taylor, David

Right: *David Taylor (left) with Alex Higgins in 1968*

David Taylor was an exceptional player who never quite realised his potential. He won the English and then World Amateur Championships in 1968 and turned professional later the same year. He performed consistently well throughout the 1970s but only reached his first major final at the 1978 UK Championship, where he lost 9-15 to Doug Mountjoy. Then Steve Davis beat him in the final of the 1981 British Open. His last major final was the 1982 Jameson International but this time Tony Knowles overcame his challenge even though he'd seen off Davis in the quarter-final.

He reached the semi-final of the World Championship in 1980 with a superb quarter-final win over six-time champion Ray Reardon, but he was beaten by eventual winner Cliff Thorburn 7-16. The following year Taylor partnered Steve Davis and John Spencer to victory in the World Team Classic, a season in which he reached a career-high seven in the world rankings.

Although his career then wound down, it was punctuated with moments of sheer brilliance: he made three consecutive total clearances and seven consecutive century breaks in exhibition matches. He then commentated on Steve Davis's first televised maximum. He was also the first player to pot all the balls in the final round of the BBC's Big Break.

Name: David Taylor
Born: July 29th 1943, Cheshire
Nationality: English
Turned Pro: 1968
Century Breaks: 12
Highest Break: 124
Ranking Titles: 0
World Titles: 0

Taylor, Dennis

Dennis Taylor made his debut at the 1973 World Championship only a year after turning professional. He was a solid break-builder and shrewd tactician, which helped him to the semi-final of the World Championship in both 1975 and 1977, but he had to wait another two years before reaching the final against debutante Terry Griffiths. The Welshman surprised everyone by winning comfortably, however, 24-16.

Taylor had a couple of quite seasons before reaching the semi-final at the Crucible in 1984. Steve Davis proved too strong however, so Taylor knuckled down on the practice table in preparation for an assault on the title the following year. He was playing well when he learned that his mother had died. Instead of giving in to grief, however, Taylor upped his game and thrashed Cliff Thorburn in the final of the 1984 Rothmans Grand Prix.

Taylor battled his way to the 1985 world final but Steve Davis was in imperious form and rattled off the first eight frames. Taylor might have capitulated but he mounted an incredible fight-back and won seven of the next eight frames. Davis held his nerve, however, and eased two frames clear, 17-15. Taylor again had to dig deep to deny Davis the single frame he needed for the match, and he eventually levelled it at 17-17.

Davis held a 62-44 lead with only the last four colours remaining, but Taylor cleared the brown, blue and pink under intense pressure to move within three points and ensure that for the first time in history the championship would go down to the final black. Eighteen million people watched the drama unfold into the night as both players repeatedly missed frame and match ball.

Then, as the clock ticked past midnight, Davis over cut the black into the corner. Taylor took an age to play it but eventually potted the black to secure his only world title. He was now a household name the world over, but he too succumbed to the Crucible Curse and was knocked out in the first round of his title defence. He recovered to win the Benson & Hedges

Right: *Dennis Taylor kisses the trophy after his epic world final against Steve Davis in 1985*

Masters in 1987.

He had a public row with Alex Higgins over Northern Ireland's performance at the 1990 World Cup, after which Higgins threatened to have him shot, although the pair eventually made up.

Taylor's career wound down in the 1990s and he dropped out of the top 16 after the 1994 World Championship. He retired in 2000 but signed up with the BBC as a commentator. He is liked and respected in equal measure for his insight, knowledge and humour.

Name: Dennis Taylor
Born: January 19th 1949, County Tyrone
Nationality: Northern Irish
Turned Pro: 1972 - 2000
Century Breaks: 63
Highest Break: 141
Ranking Titles: 2
World Titles: 1

Thorburn

Above: *Cliff 'The Grinder' Thorburn*

Having met John Spencer in Canada, Cliff Thorburn came to England in the early 1970s to play professional snooker. He made an immediate impact and was runner-up to Spencer in the 1977 World Championship. Three years later he made the world final for the second time. The two finalists could hardly have been more different: Alex Higgins was the volatile and temperamental genius, Thorburn the meticulous plodder who could knuckle down and get on with the job. Thorburn eventually ground out an 18-16 victory and moved to number two in the world.

The following season he reached the top spot and was made a Member of the Order of Canada. He then became the first player to make a maximum at the Crucible during his second round match against Terry Griffiths at the 1983 championship. He won the match 13-12 and then squeezed past compatriot Kirk Stevens by the same score. He beat Tony Knowles in the semi (16-15), with the match finishing at 2.30am. He was then given the terrible news that his wife had suffered a miscarriage. Quite understandably he wasn't at his best and went down 6-18 to Steve Davis in the final.

Thorburn was Masters champion three times (1983, 1985 and 1986), and he also defeated Davis en route to the Rothmans Grand Prix in 1984/85, although he lost to Dennis Taylor in the final. He was runner-up to Willie Thorne (8-13) at the 1985 Mercantile Credit Classic, and was runner-up again the following year to Jimmy White (12-13). He made up for these final losses by winning the Scottish Masters both years. He was then banned for two ranking tournaments for failing a dope test.

His career gradually petered out and he made it to the Crucible for the last time in 1994. He led Nigel Bond 9-2 in their opening match but somehow contrived to lose 10-9. He returned to the UK in 2010 to compete on the legends' tour.

Name: Cliff Thorburn
Born: January 16th 1948, Victoria
Nationality: Canadian
Turned Pro: 1972 - 1996
Century Breaks: 74
Highest Break: 147
Ranking Titles: 2
World Titles: 1

Thorne

Right: *Willie Thorne sizes up the balls*

Willie Thorne never quite realised his potential. On the practice table he regularly knocked in maximum breaks but couldn't convert his considerable talent into tournament victories. He won the National Under-16 Title in 1970 but waited five years before turning professional. He had to wait another seven years before making an impact at the World Championship when he made the quarter-final in 1982.

He peaked in 1985 when he won the ranking Classic event, and later that year he reached the final of the prestigious UK Championship. He built an impressive 13-8 lead over Steve Davis and only needed to knock in a simple blue off its spot to take a practically unassailable lead, but he took his eye off the pot and handed Davis a lifeline. Davis duly recovered and won the title, 16-14. Thorne put the defeat behind him, however, and made the quarter-final of the 1986 World Championship.

Thorne struggled throughout the remainder of the decade with a serious gambling problem. He once laid £38,000 on John Parrott to lose after the latter had lost his cue and had to make do with one provided by the venue. Thorne commentated on the match and had to bite his tongue when Parrott won. He also regularly placed £20,000 bets on horse races.

He may have knocked in over 200 maximums in practice but he had to wait until the 1987 UK Championship to register one in competitive play. His career then wound down, although he regularly competed on the senior tour and is now valued for his entertaining and insightful commentary on television.

Name: Willie Thorne
Born: March 4th 1954, Leicester
Nationality: English
Turned Pro: 1975 - 2002
Century Breaks: 126
Highest Break: 147
Ranking Titles: 1
World Titles: 0

Trump

Judd Trump is one of a new breed of exciting young players who looks set to remain at the top of the game for the next generation. He was English Under-13 and Under-14 Champion and he reached the World Under-21 semi-final aged 14. He then became the youngest player to make a competitive 147.

Trump joined the professional tour in 2005 and immediately became the youngest player to qualify for the final stages of a ranking tournament (Welsh Open). He then became the third youngest person (after Stephen Hendry and Ronnie O'Sullivan) to play at the Crucible during the 2007 World Championship. He led Shaun Murphy 6-5 but eventually lost 6-10.

He then had a quiet year before raising his profile with wins over Joe Perry and Ronnie O'Sullivan at the Grand Prix, and then Mark Williams in qualifying for the 2008 Bahrain Championship. By the end of the year he was in the world's top 32. He had to wait another couple of years before reaching his first ranking final, the 2011 China open, where he beat Mark Selby 10-8 to claim the title.

He then beat defending champion Neil Robertson in the first round of the World Championship. He backed this up with wins over Martin Gould, Graeme Dott and Ding Junhui in subsequent rounds to set up a final against John Higgins, although he lost a tight encounter 15-18.

Above: *Judd Trump with the 2011 UK Championship trophy*

In December 2011 he beat Dominic Dale, O'Sullivan, Stephen Maguire, Neil Robertson and Mark Allen to win his second ranking event at the UK Championship, and he then reached the semi-final of the Masters. Three ranking quarter-finals followed and he moved up to number two in the world. He had a disappointing 2012 World Championship, however, and let a 12-9 second-round lead over Ali Carter slip, denying him the

Right: *Rising superstar Judd Trump (left) with avid fan, Ollie Gammond*

chance to move to world number one.

He should have beaten John Higgins in the final of the Shanghai Masters but threw away a 7-2 lead. He recovered to win the inaugural International Championship and claim the number one spot. He then reached the final of the Premier League and the semi-final of the Welsh Open. He made it to the semi-final of the 2013 World Championship but couldn't trouble Ronnie O'Sullivan and eventually lost 11-17.

Trump is a flair player who entertains crowds with his style and speed around the table. He looks set to challenge some of the records set by the greats of the modern era: O'Sullivan, Hendry, Higgins and Davis.

Name: Judd Trump
Born: August 21st 1989, Bristol
Nationality: English
Turned Pro: 2005
Century Breaks: 217
Highest Break: 144
Ranking Titles: 3
World Titles: 0

Virgo

John Virgo didn't turn professional until he was 30, but, with the likes of Ray Reardon, Eddie Charlton and John Spencer still on the circuit, he was one of a new style of player. Three years later he reached the semi-final of the World Championship at the Crucible but he was beaten 12-19 by Dennis Taylor. Later that year he won the prestigious UK Championship against the then World Champion, Terry Griffiths, although he was docked two frames for missing the scheduled start time and the tournament wasn't a ranking event. In 1980 he broke into the world's top 10 and he was a consistent performer over much of the next decade.

Virgo is well known for his impressions of other players and his wide variety of trick shots. When the semi-finals of the 1982 and 1985 World Championships finished early, Virgo performed a routine aping Alex Higgins, Terry Griffiths and Dennis Taylor.

He retired in 1995 to concentrate on presenting the BBC's snooker game show, Big Break, which ran until 2002. He also wrote a tribute to Alex Higgins and a number of books on his repertoire of trick shots.

Above: *John Virgo (left) and Jimmy White entertain the crowd*

Name: John Virgo
Born: March 3rd 1946, Salford
Nationality: English
Turned Pro: 1976 - 1995
Century Breaks: 26
Highest Break: 139
Ranking Titles: 0
World Titles: 0

Walden

Below: *Ricky Walden at the 2011 Paul Hunter Classic*

Ricky Walden started on the minor UK tour in 1999 and graduated to the main tour two years later. In his first year he beat John Higgins at the Grand Prix and the UK Championship and climbed 30 places to world number 48. He also reached the quarter-final of the China Open, but he had to wait until 2008 before securing his first ranking title, the Shanghai Masters. He had to win two qualifying matches to make the tournament proper but then showed his class by beating Stephen Hendry, Neil Robertson, Steve Davis and Mark Selby to set up a final against Ronnie O'Sullivan. He finally overcame O'Sullivan 10-8 but the remainder of his season was uncharacteristically quiet.

Having been knocked out in the first round at his first World Championship, he qualified as a seeded player in 2011, but he again came up short at the Crucible against Rory McLeod. He then had a quiet patch before beating Stephen Lee, Mark Williams and Shaun Murphy at the UK Championships to set up a semi-final against Mark Allen. Walden made the better start but he eventually lost 7-9. He played in all 12 of the PTC events but only reached one final (which he lost to Neil Robertson), although he did manage a 147 during Event 10. Despite failing to qualify for the 2012 World Championships, he finished the season ranked 15 in the world.

His 2012/13 season began well with wins over Zhu Yinghui, Joe Perry, Robert Milkins and Marcus Campbell at the ranking Wuxi Classic. In the final, opponent Stuart Bingham knocked in a 147 but he couldn't prevent Walden from winning his second ranking title. He was then dumped out of the UK Championship by 17-year-old Luca Brecel in the first round. He bounced back with a superb run to the semi-final of the 2013 World Championship, although he couldn't squeeze past Barry Hawkins.

Name: Ricky Walden
Born: November 11th 1982, Chester
Nationality: English
Turned Pro: 1999
Century Breaks: 141
Highest Break: 147
Ranking Titles: 2
World Titles: 0

Wattana

James Wattana won the Thailand Masters in 1986 when he was only 16. He then won the World Amateur Championship and turned professional. He was a force throughout the 1990s, winning the Thailand Open twice and climbing to number three in the world rankings. He knocked in his first maximum at the 1991 World Masters, and his second the following year at the British Open.

Wattana is rightly credited with popularising the game in the Far East, and the likes of Marco Fu and Ding Junhui owe much of their success to Wattana's willingness to take on and beat the established Europeans. In 1993 he reached the semi-final of the World Championship after wins over Tony Jones, Steve James and John Parrott. Four years later he knocked in his third maximum (on the day his father died) on his way to another Crucible semi-final.

His career then gradually wound down and he slipped outside the top 32. He bounced back in 2004/05 but then dropped off the main tour in 2008. He returned in 2009 after winning the Asian Championships, and he then reached the finals of the China Open to secure his place on the tour.

Above: *Thai superstar James Wattana*

Name: James Wattana
Born: January 17th 1970, Bangkok
Nationality: Thai
Turned Pro: 1989
Century Breaks: 149
Highest Break: 147
Ranking Titles: 3
World Titles: 0

Wenbo

Right: *Liang Wenbo is another Chinese player looking to make his mark on the sport*

Liang Wenbo enjoyed a solid amateur career and took a team gold medal at the 2006 Asian Games. Having then won the 2005 World Under-21 Championship he received a wildcard to join the main tour. He immediately qualified for the Welsh Open and thrashed Nigel Bond 5-0 in his opening match, although he was then knocked out by Graeme Dott. Subsequent poor performances saw him ranked a lowly 78, and he struggled in qualifying for the next two seasons.

He finally qualified for the 2008 Northern Ireland Trophy and then beat Steve Davis and Peter Ebdon to reach the last 16. He was knocked out in the next round by John Higgins but moved up to 26 in the world rankings. He made a 147 in qualifying for the Bahrain Championship but then lost to Michael Judge. He also lost to compatriot Ding Junhui in the first round at the Crucible.

He improved in 2009 and beat world number two Stephen Maguire to win the Beijing Challenge. He then finished runner-up to Ronnie O'Sullivan at the Shanghai Masters. His good form continued and he reached the quarter-final of the UK Championship as well as qualifying again for the World Championships, results that elevated him to the top 16.

He dropped out of the elite group after a poor 2010/11 season but then he and Ding won the World Cup. However, a number of low finishes culminated in a narrow first-round defeat to John Higgins at the 2012 World Championships.

Name: Liang Wenbo
Born: March 5th 1987, Zhaodong
Nationality: Chinese
Turned Pro: 2004
Century Breaks: 91
Highest Break: 147
Ranking Titles: 0
World Titles: 0

Werbeniuk

Big Bill Werbeniuk slowly climbed the world rankings until he peaked at number eight in 1983. But his progress was hindered by a tremor in his arm that often caused him to miss shots. He counteracted the involuntary movement by consuming alcohol in enormous quantities – usually six pints of lager before a match and then at least another pint per frame. He reportedly drank 30 pints and then eight double whiskies during a particularly long match.

He reached the quarter-final of the World Championship four times but his alcohol intake was impacting his health so he turned to propranolol to help look after his heart. Later in his career, this beta-blocker was banned by International Olympic Committee as a performance-enhancing drug and this ruling was then adopted by World Snooker. Werbeniuk protested that it was for legitimate medicinal use but he was fined and sanctioned anyway. He retired from snooker in 1990 and took up pool, which didn't have the drug on its banned list, to try to clear his debts.

Werbeniuk was larger than life in every sense, and his good humour – he once split his trousers stretching for a difficult shot at the Crucible – and dazzling skills were sorely missed. He died of heart failure a few days after his 56th birthday.

Left: *Big Bill Werbeniuk*

Name: Bill Werbeniuk
Born: January 14th 1947, Winnipeg
Died: January 20th 2003, Vancouver
Nationality: Canadian
Turned Pro: 1973 - 1990
Century Breaks: 15
Highest Break: 147
Ranking Titles: 0
World Titles: 0

White

Jimmy White often played truant from school so he could head down to the local snooker hall and practice. He was a prodigiously talented youngster and he won the English Amateur Championship in 1979. The following year he became the youngest winner of the World Amateur Championship.

He first qualified for the Crucible in 1981 but it was to be a venue that would haunt him. He won the Scottish Masters and Northern Ireland Classic leading up to the 1982 World Championship and was leading Alex Higgins 15-14 in their semi-final at the tournament when he missed a red with the rest. Higgins cleared up and then took the deciding frame.

Two years later White won the Masters and then reached his first world final. Steve Davis raced into a 12-4 lead but White fought back and only needed another couple of pots to take the match into a deciding frame. He could not force home his advantage, however, and Davis won an epic match 18-16. He recovered quickly and teamed up with Alex Higgins to take the World Doubles Title.

White secured several ranking victories – the Irish Masters, the Grand Prix and the British Open to name but three – before falling at the final hurdle against Davis in the 1987 UK Championship. He also reached another couple of world semi-finals and peaked at number two in the rankings.

White avenged some of the disappointments by beating Davis 16-14 in the semi-final of the 1990 World Championship, but he lost the final 12-18 to Stephen Hendry. White again overcame the disappointment and won three titles on the bounce: the World Matchplay and the 1991 Classic against Hendry, and the World Masters against Tony Drago.

With Hendry succumbing to the Crucible Curse, White was finally expected to be crowned World Champion in 1991 and he duly reached the final, only to be beaten by John Parrott. Parrott also beat him in the final of the UK Championship later in the year. He began the 1992 World Championship in blistering form and knocked in only the second maximum at the event, and he then opened up a six-frame advantage over Hendry in the final (14-8). But then White began to unravel and a series of misses and the odd slice of misfortune saw Hendry win 10 consecutive frames and take the title.

He proved himself a terrific fighter by winning the Grand Prix and the UK Championship, but his form going into the 1993 World Championships was patchy. He battled his way to the final but was once again beaten by his nemesis, Hendry running away with it and winning 18-5 with a session to spare.

Another quiet season culminated in yet another barnstorming run at the Crucible and he met Hendry in the final for the fourth time in five years. The match ebbed and flowed and the pair were eventually tied with 17 frames apiece. White looked certain to take the match when he missed a simple black off its spot. Hendry cleared up and took the title, although White, as ever, was gracious in defeat: "He's beginning to annoy me."

White's form took another dip when he underwent treatment for testicular cancer, but he somehow managed to reach another semi-final at the Crucible. Hendry again stood in his way, however, and the Scotsman prevailed 16-12. His form then dropped away and he fell out of the world's top 16 in 1997.

He regained his place among the world's elite after making the semi of the 1997 Grand Prix and the quarter-final of the 1998 World Championship. His form was patchy over the following seasons with several good finishes interspersed among early exits. He then rolled back the years with big wins over Neil Robertson, Stephen Hendry and Peter Ebdon to reach the semi-final of the 2004 Masters, and he proved this was no flash in the pan by then winning the Players' Championship, his first ranking title in more than a decade.

However, he dropped out of the top 32 in 2006 and only qualified for one ranking event in 2007 (the China Open). He continued to slide down the rankings until he won the 6-red World Grand Prix in 2009. He went on to win the World Series of Snooker in Prague and the World Seniors' Championship but these victories couldn't hide the fact that his career was on a downward spiral. He is currently ranked 57.

White is well liked by the snooker establishment and his flamboyant playing style and never-say-die attitude ensure he remains popular with a huge fan base that rivals that of Ronnie O'Sullivan.

Name: Jimmy White, MBE
Born: May 2nd 1952, Tooting
Nationality: English
Turned Pro: 1980
Century Breaks: 291
Highest Break: 147
Ranking Titles: 10
World Titles: 0

Wilkinson

Left: *Gary Wilkinson*

Far Left: *Jimmy White is probably the best player with the rest*

Having joined the professional tour in 1987, Gary Wilkinson quickly climbed the rankings to world number five by 1991. He reached four major semi-finals and the final of that year's British Open – as well as the Scottish Masters – but he never managed to win a ranking event. He came through the qualifying tournament for the Crucible eight times, a record only bettered by John Parrott, but his best performances came in 1991 and 1995 when he reached the quarter-finals.

He won the non-ranking World Matchplay in 1992 and managed to stay in the top 32 for most of the decade but he then slipped down the rankings and ended up working as a tournament assistant for the sport's governing body.

Name: Gary Wilkinson
Born: April 7th 1966
Nationality: English
Turned Pro: 1987
Century Breaks: 66
Highest Break: 139
Ranking Titles: 0
World Titles: 0

Williams, Mark

Mark Williams won his first junior event aged 11 and made his first century at 13. He worked briefly in the mines and was a promising schoolboy boxer but he chose snooker instead and turned professional in 1992. He broke into the elite top 16 after only three years, and he took his first ranking title – the Welsh Open – in 1996.

Williams's career took off and he won the 1996 Grand Prix, the 1997 British Open and the 1998 Masters. In between times, he also reached the last 16 of the 1997 World Championship, the semi-final in 1998 and the final in 1999 (where he was beaten by Stephen Hendry).

His good form continued with a win at the 1999 UK Championship and stirring 17-15 and 18-16 victories over John Higgins and compatriot Matthew Stevens respectively to take the 2000 world title. These performances saw him ranked number one in the world, which he cemented with victory at the subsequent Grand Prix. He was another to succumb to the Crucible Curse, however, as he went down 12-13 to Joe Swail in the second round.

He rediscovered his form in 2002/03 by winning the UK Championship, the Masters and his second World Championship, the latter after an epic fight-back from Ken Doherty had seen the Irishman level at 16 frames apiece having been 10-2 behind.

In 2005 he became the fifth person to knock in a maximum at the Crucible, but he had to wait another year before claiming his 16th ranking title at the China Open. His next season was a poor one and he dropped out of the top 16 until 2009. He didn't recover his form until taking the China Open in 2010, by which time he was back in the top 16. He then reached the final of the UK Championship, although John Higgins edged him out 10-9. He bounced back and won

Left: *Mark Williams*

the ranking German Masters before progressing to the semi-final of the World Championship. Although John Higgins again proved too strong, Williams regained the number one spot after Selby's early exit. However, his form then nosedived and he considered retirement.

Name: Mark Williams
Born: March 21st 1975, Ebbw Vale
Nationality: Welsh
Turned Pro: 1992
Century Breaks: 290
Highest Break: 147
Ranking Titles: 18
World Titles: 2

Williams, Rex

Right: *Rex Williams*

Rex Williams was an excellent junior but he turned professional when both snooker and billiards were in serious decline. He came up against John Pulman in the world final in 1964 and 1965 but was beaten both times. The following year he became the second man (after Joe Davis) to make a confirmed 147.

He turned his attention to billiards and won seven world titles between 1968 and 1983, and he also reached the semi-final of the World Snooker Championship in 1972 (he was beaten by Alex Higgins having been four frames up with five to play). He lost again at the same stage to Graham Miles in 1974.

In 1986 Williams became the oldest man (53) to reach a ranking final, although he lost to Jimmy White at the Rothmans Grand Prix. He was also instrumental in dragging snooker in to the modern, professional age as chairman of the WPBSA from 1968 to 1987 and 1997 to 1999. He was accidentally expelled in 2001 but was reinstated the following year. He was also a popular and knowledgeable commentator during the 1980s.

Name: Rex Williams
Born: July 20th 1933, Halesowen
Nationality: English
Turned Pro: 1951 - 1994
Century Breaks: 14
Highest Break: 147
Ranking Titles: 0
World Titles: 0

Woollaston

Ben Woollaston started on the Challenge Tour in 2003 and enjoyed a brief spell on the main tour two years later. Having dropped off, he returned after winning the European Under-19 Championship. He then reached the tournament proper of the 2007 Welsh Open having come through qualifying but he was beaten by Stephen Hendry in the second round.

He won his first pro title by beating Graeme Dott at Event 3 of the PTC in 2011/12 but he then lost in the Finals to Ding Junhui, with the Chinese also beating him in the China Open. He climbed 26 places during the season – the most by anyone on the professional circuit – and is now ranked world number 35.

Name: Ben Woollaston
Born: May 14th 1987, Leicester
Nationality: English
Turned Pro: 2003
Century Breaks: 39
Highest Break: 145
Ranking Titles: 0
World Titles: 0

Above: *Ben Woollaston*

ALSO AVAILABLE IN THE PLAYER BY PLAYER SERIES

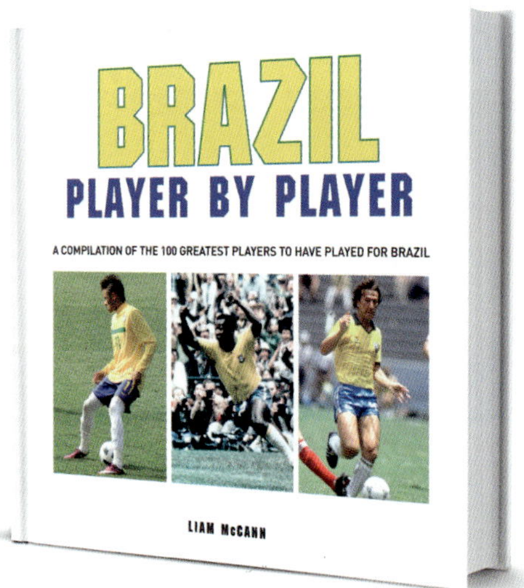

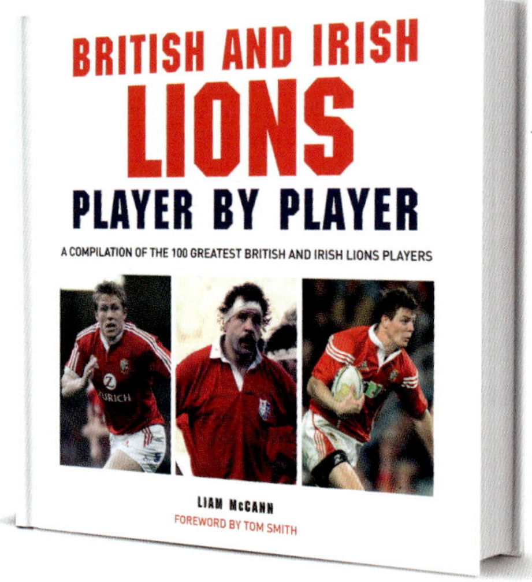

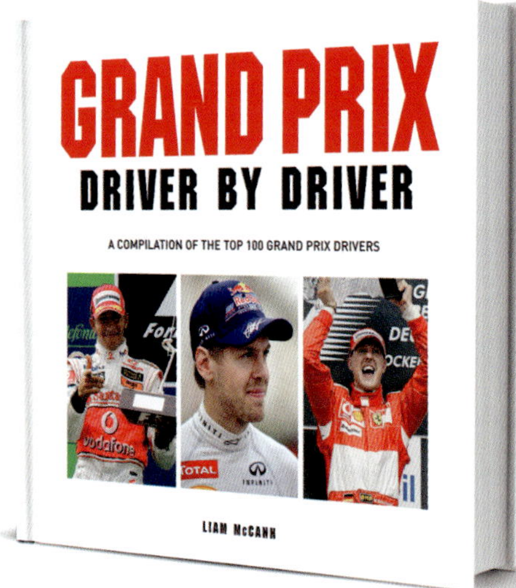

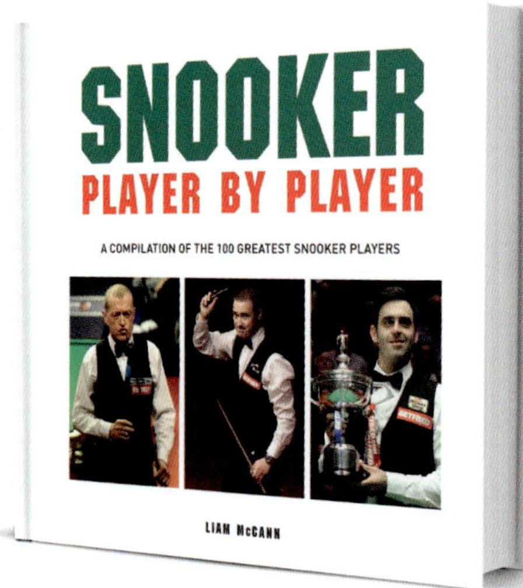

ALSO AVAILABLE IN THE PLAYER BY PLAYER SERIES

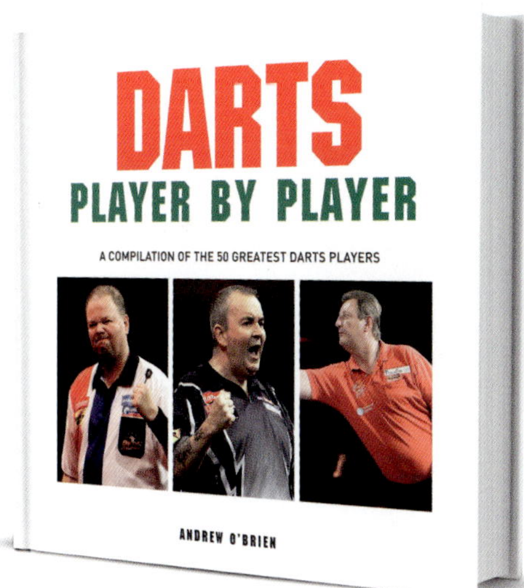

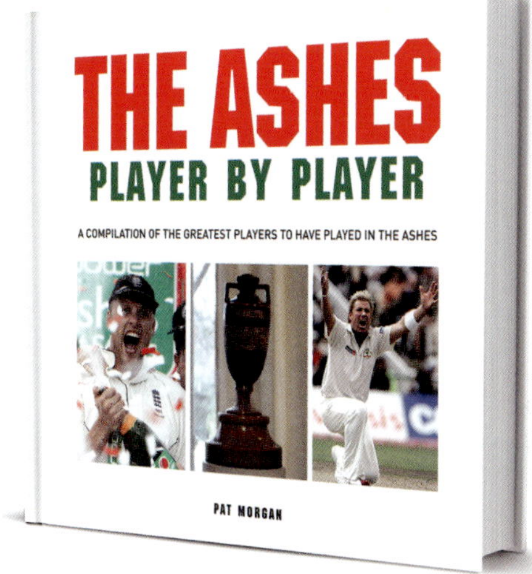

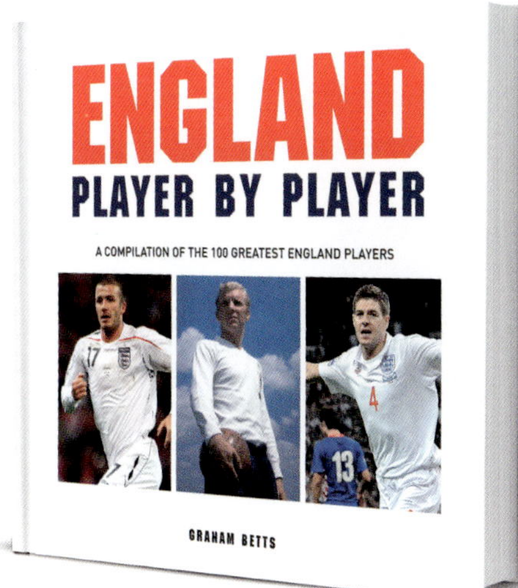

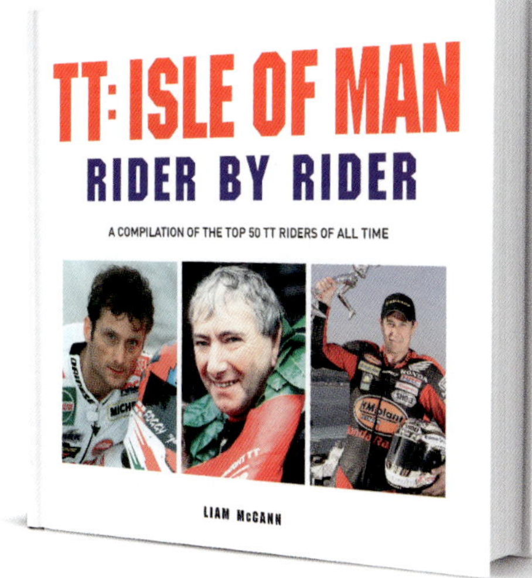

The pictures in this book were provided courtesy of the following:

GETTY IMAGES
101 Bayham Street, London NW1 0AG

WIKICOMMONS
commons.wikimedia.org

Design & Artwork by: Scott Giarnese & Alex Young

Published by: Demand Media Limited & G2 Entertainment Limited

Publishers: Jason Fenwick & Jules Gammond

Written by: Liam McCann